POETRY COMI

GREAT MINDS

Your World...Your Future...YOUR WORDS

From North West England
Vol I

Edited by Steve Twelvetree

 Young**Writers**

First published in Great Britain in 2005 by:
Young Writers
Remus House
Coltsfoot Drive
Peterborough
PE2 9JX
Telephone: 01733 890066
Website: www.youngwriters.co.uk

SB I SBN 1 84460 881 6

Foreword

This year, the Young Writers' 'Great Minds' competition proudly presents a showcase of the best poetic talent selected from over 40,000 up-and-coming writers nationwide.

Young Writers was established in 1991 to promote the reading and writing of poetry within schools and to the youth of today. Our books nurture and inspire confidence in the ability of young writers and provide a snapshot of poems written in schools and at home by budding poets of the future.

The thought, effort, imagination and hard work put into each poem impressed us all and the task of selecting poems was a difficult but nevertheless enjoyable experience.

We hope you are as pleased as we are with the final selection and that you and your family continue to be entertained with *Great Minds From North West England Vol I* for many years to come.

Contents

Martin Hawes (11)   49
Adam Laycock (11)   50
Sam Cook (11)   50
Nicholas Johnston (12)   51
Luke Glover (12)   51
Joe Callaghan (11)   52
Rory Woodward (11)   53
Yousaf Ibrahim (11)   53
Jack Hartley (12)   54
Liam Townsend (11)   54

Burscough Priory Science College, Burscough

Lauren Wilkinson (13)   55
Cameron McFarlane (12)   55
Mark Huyton (12)   56
Chloe Dorrian (12)   57
Cathy Ingham (13)   58
Louise Boardman (12)   58
Bethany Richards (12)   59
Stephen Hayter (12)   59
Georgina Hales (12)   60
Craig Kewley (13)   61
Alexander Bailey (13)   62
Thomas Virtue (12)   62
Hannah Griggs (12)   63
Jessica Waring-Hughes (12)   63
Sarah Lygo (13)   64
Nathan Davies (12)   65
Francesca Bailey (12)   66
Amy Lea (12)   67
Tayla Murphy (12)   67
Rebecca Williams (12)   68
Katy Taylor (12)   69
Daniel Bradshaw (12)   70
Hannah Nicholson (13)   71
Rachel Hesketh (12)   71
Alice Gradwell (12)   72
Melissa Bailey (12)   73
Jessica Dixon (12)   73
Jessica Mooney (12)   74
Cameron Cox (12)   75

Hannah Brocken (12)	76
Alex Noon (12)	77
Sophie Hill (12)	78
Teddi Forshaw (13)	78
Alexander Cooke (12)	79
Hayley Wareing (12)	80
Rachel Bunting (12)	81
Laura Baldwin (13)	82
Emily Farley (12)	83
Vanessa Lamb (12)	84
Oliver Howarth (12)	85
Lauren Kelly (12)	86
Jennifer Scully (12)	87
James Seddon (13)	88
Sean Howard (12)	89
Dale Cheetham (12)	90
Zoe Bober (12)	91
Nicole Dawson (13)	92
Wendy Walker (13)	93
Georgina Richards (12)	94
Samantha Holden (12)	95
Rachel Fenelon (12)	96
Rebecca Kite (12)	97
Gemma Knell (12)	98
James Power (12)	99
Aliki Panteli (12)	100
Emma Binns (12)	101
Nicola Jerath (13)	102
Jenny Evans (12)	103
Holly Rothwell (12)	104
Emma Craddock (12)	105
Alex Rhodes (12)	106
Bethan Caine (12)	107

Ellesmere Port Catholic High School, Ellesmere Port

Jack Jones (12)	107
Rebecca Hart (11)	108
Jessica Hulse (12)	108
Alex Wasley (12)	109
Ben Cameron (12)	109
Clare Nuttall (11)	110

Emma Williams (12)	111
Georgina Jones (11)	111
Gregory Marsland (12)	112
Natalie Harding (13)	113
Laura Tolley (12)	114
Darcy Siegertsz (13)	114
Thomas Fildes (12)	115
Andrew Henry (12)	115
Adam Middleton (12)	116
Latiffa Cliffe (12)	116
Sophie McDonald (12)	117
Susannah Brumby (11)	117
Laura Abbate (11)	118
Conor Gilmour (11)	118
Nathan Watson (12)	119
Grace Taylor (11)	119
Daniel Smith (12)	120
Robert Jones (12)	120
Shaun Mander (11)	120
Sarah Warren (13)	121
Claire Craven (12)	121
Krystal Watson (11)	121
Natalie Poole (11)	122
Rebecca Birchall (11)	122
Lucy McVeigh (12)	122
Charlotte Gray (13)	123
Jade Griffiths (11)	123
Lewis Dodson (12)	124

Frodsham Science & Technology College, Frodsham

Lyndsey Weeks (13)	125
Nicola Cunningham (13)	126
Andy Perrin (12)	126
Jennie Hooper (13)	127
Laura Lunny (13)	127
Sammir Radha (13)	128
Ben Davies (13)	129
Stephen Smith (14)	130
Katy Ingram (13)	130
Emily Hignell (14)	131
Jack Wilson (11)	131

Melissa McGowan (14)   132
Laura Berry (13)   132
Jake Hardman (14)   133
Rachelle Carter-Shepherd (14)   133
Daniel Pacheco (14)   134
Joshua Solari (13)   134
Ameira-Louise Hasoun (13)   135
Dean Ratcliffe (13)   136
Daniel Collinson (13)   137
Alex MacGugan (14)   137
Gareth Miller (14)   138
Katie Stubbs (13)   138
Jake Garner (14)   139
Alex Flood (14)   139
Ashleigh Fry (13)   140
Rachel Foreman (13)   141
Jenna Johnston (15)   142
Zara Gerrard (13)   143
Joshua Kennils (11)   143
Hannah Pierce (13)   144
Steph Oscroft (17)   145
Robert Ward-Dutton (13)   146
Johanna Pickering (14)   147

Mostyn House School, South Wirral

Amy Hammond (11)   148
Lauren Morgan (11)   148

New Heys Comprehensive School, Liverpool

Rebecca Hanmer & Rachel McDonald (11)   149
Vicky Williams (14)   149
Alice Williams (11)   150
Amy Green (12)   150
Paul Roberts (14)   151
Rebecca Blackall (11)   151
Craig Dineley (14)   152
Laura Tickle (12)   152
Cara McPartland (11)   153
Hannah Langley (11)   153
Kelly Walker (11)   154
Lucy Roberts (12)   154

Jessica Thorpe (12)	176
Danielle Gubb (12)	176
Christopher Brennan (14)	177
Rachel Clear (12)	177
Sarah Chialton (12)	178
Sarah Gardam (13)	178
Steven Milward (12)	179

Sacred Heart Catholic High School, Liverpool
Callum Johnstone (12)	179
Natalie J Romero (12)	180
Sean Seasman (13)	181

Sale Grammar School, Sale
Jack Cartwright (11)	181
Thomas Powell (12)	182
Stephanie Hong (11)	182
Adam Legg (11)	183
Andrew Carson (11)	183
Calum Clarke (13)	184
Ben Stokes (11)	184
Jack Marsland (11)	185
Olivia Al-Noah (11)	185
Charlotte Lamb (11)	186
Beth Aulton (12)	187
Andrew Wilson (12)	188
Aisha Baden (11)	189
Sophie Wheeler (12)	190
Ben Hughes (11)	190
Michael Savage (12)	191
Andrew Aylott (11)	191
Sarah Turner (13)	192
Nicholas Bell (11)	193
Mohamed Zardab (11)	194
Jonathan Clarke (11)	194
Craig Kitchener (11)	195
Charlotte Mapp (11)	195
Daniel Fisher (11)	196
Bethany Cooper (11)	196
Michael Hopkins (11)	197
Kara Wilson (11)	197

The Belvedere School, Liverpool

The Blue Coat School, Liverpool

The Poems

Summer

After Spring had come
And treated the Earth as its mother
The world was welcomed by Sun
And was making way for Summer

She prowled over the Earth like a cat
Bringing light to the darkest places
She smiled to the seasons and said, 'Beat that!'
She looked at the smiles on our faces

Afterwards her power was dying
And Autumn soon took her place
And the people of Earth started crying
Wishing they would see her face.

Jennifer Jardine (11)
Abbey Gate College, Chester

Mr Winter

A man strode in white and cold
Making cars steam up
And treacherous roads

A man strode in white and cold
Making animals sleepy
And ravenous crows

A man strode in white and cold
Making Jesus on the donkey
Have frozen toes

A man strode up white and cold
Being stopped by Spring, the bouncer
And thrown on the road.

George Bryant (11)
Abbey Gate College, Chester

Seasons

The winter nights are slow
Days go flashing by.
The snow falls
And snowmen come and go.

Spring comes racing forward,
The leaves begin to show,
The suncream comes out of hibernation,
The blossom continues to grow.

Summer nights are quick,
Summer days are hot,
We are going on a holiday,
To the beach we go a lot.

Autumn just arriving,
It is a new term at school,
It is getting quite cold,
After the leaves begin to fall.

Thomas Dickinson (11)
Abbey Gate College, Chester

The Best Holiday

Holidays, holidays
Are so much fun.
I love getting a tan in the sun.
Suncream on, rub it around,
Doing handstands on the ground.
Postcards sent to a friend,
I don't want this holiday to end.

The end comes
And your suitcase weighs tonnes,
I'm feeling sad, I'm feeling glum,
But I can't wait 'til next year's fun.

Rochelle Harman (11)
Abbey Gate College, Chester

My Dog

My dog is white, we've had him a while
My dog is great, he's the best by a mile
He's not very fast and he's full of greed
He's always waiting for his next feed

He was born overseas and is used to being hot
He's much better here though and enjoys it a lot
My dog is fab, my dog is cool
But sometimes he acts like a complete fool

Some people think he doesn't look handsome
He's a bull terrier and worth a king's ransom
His face is gorgeous, the best we've seen
He's all-round perfect and we call him Dean.

Robert Marks (11)
Abbey Gate College, Chester

The Moon

The moon is a piece of foil
On a black baking tray

It is a torch
In a dark room

The moon is the light
Shining on a polished shoe

It is a white button
On a black coat

The moon is a silver buckle
On a black belt.

Josh Williams (11)
Abbey Gate College, Chester

The Moon Is . . .

The moon is,
A bulb placed in a dark room being turned on and off.

It is chalk,
Being rubbed on a blackboard.

The moon is,
A piece of paper being dropped into a murky puddle.

It is,
A round football being thrown up in the air.

The moon is,
A piece of cloth being hung up in the warm night.

Charlotte Graves (11)
Abbey Gate College, Chester

Sense Of Summer

Summer's first breath
Dances through the canopies.
Trees tingle with excitement
At their old friend's return.

Drifting through the air
Summer's full fragrance.
Insects lazing in the thermals
Cats basking in the sun.

Smiling sunflowers softly sway,
Bees burdened with sweet pollen,
Buzz and bumble through the day,
Like small angels come from Heaven.

Barbecues beneath bat-filled skies,
The sound of children in their element.
Pink and purple summer nights,
Golden glowing sunsets.

Georgina Gardner Stockley (11)
Abbey Gate College, Chester

What Is The Moon?

The moon is a silver piece of glitter
On a black strand of hair.

It is a white drop of milk
On a black table.

It is a white stone
In a muddy puddle.

The moon is a silver ring
On a black sheet of paper.

It is a white ball
On a black picnic rug.

The moon is a white piece of paper
In the bottom of a black bin.

It is a white clock
On a black wall.

Christina Ioannou (12)
Abbey Gate College, Chester

What Is The Moon?

The moon is a plate
On a navy table cloth

It is a light bulb
In a dark room

The moon is a face
Looking through the curtains

It is a white ball
Floating in dark water

The moon is a standing-out dot
On my woolly black jumper.

Polijne Willemse (11)
Abbey Gate College, Chester

Socks

Socks are fun,
Socks are cool.
You can wear them to work,
You can wear them to school.

Socks are smelly,
Socks are great.
Socks are a friend,
Socks are a mate.

Socks are top!
If you think they are bad,
Then you get smiling
'Cause you must be quite sad.

Socks get wet,
Socks get lost.
Socks keep you warm
In the morning frost.

Socks keep me warm inside my shoe,
Socks keep my feet from turning blue.

Bethany McLoughlin (11)
Abbey Gate College, Chester

Hitchhiker

The hitchhiker standing there,
Pick him up if you dare!
Thumb up, drive past,
He'll still be there.
Not like *you* care!
He could jog after you,
Don't worry you can sue!
Could you be a little kinder?
Pick him up and here's a reminder!
Just imagine you were him,
But obviously you're not and
Wouldn't dream of it!

Gareth Jones (11)
Abbey Gate College, Chester

The Rain

I look out of my window
at the rain coming down.
I can hear the little raindrops
and see the leaves that drown.

Puddles of water
like little seas
and drip, drop, drip, drop
coming from the trees.

The raindrops fall
like tears from the sky.
I look up and wonder
and ask myself why.

The little drops of miracles
that have fallen from the sky.
I can hear the little raindrops
and hear the wind's cry.

Lucy Fenton (11)
Abbey Gate College, Chester

My Dog

I come home and he greets me
I love the way he meets me
He jumps up, I ruffle his fur
He does a mad lap round the kitchen

I pick him up and put him outside
He watches the slugs as they slide
When it gets cold he scratches and cries
So I let him in and he gets dry

I feed him dog meat
And sometimes he has a treat
He's six months old, white and fluffy
And he's called Alfie!

Jack Donald (11)
Abbey Gate College, Chester

What's Behind My Door?

When I was only two years old,
I was lying in bed feeling poorly and sick.
My temperature rose to one hundred and four,
When I heard a terrifying thud at my door.

Oh no, it was the monster!
The monster from under the stairs,
The one with the slimy claw
And there he was waiting outside my door.

My brother told me he'd seen the monster too.
He described him as ten feet tall,
With a head as big as a boar
And there he was shaking the knob on my door.

My temperature is dropping by the second,
I am starting to feel myself again.
Pulling the bed sheets from my head, I'm not afraid anymore.
I look over and see . . .
My *mum* standing at my door.

Rebecca Haslam (11)
Abbey Gate College, Chester

The Beach

I'm stretched out sleepily in the shade,
When the sun is as hot as it can be.
It's really hot as I have a glass of lemonade
And I feel I can see as far as the sea.

The sea looks like a huge carpet of water,
As I run towards it for a swim,
But the sand is as hot as a 90° sauna,
So I run as if I was an Olympic runner.

I'm so glad to reach the sea,
I splash about like a dog with a stick.
As the tiny waves welcome me
And I feel as cool as a mountain stream.

John Oliver Williams (11)
Abbey Gate College, Chester

Missing

Jack went missing yesterday,
Miss got really worried.
He was missing for maths and for English
And later, even for play.

Miss got in a right flurry,
For we had a geography exam.
She said we needed to start soon
And that he'd better get back in a hurry.

He'd been missing for four hours, when,
Miss said we'd better have a look.
She sent Millie off to the cloakroom
And Jamie off to the playpen.

Jack went missing yesterday,
Miss got really worried.
It turned out he was feeling poorly
And would be back the very next day.

Elizabeth Nock (11)
Abbey Gate College, Chester

The Sea

The sea can be a cause of death
Yet it could save your life
You can make a living from it
Or just have some fun
It can be home to millions of things
Like sharks and their teeth
And skate with their wings
Or be a holiday resort where
Kids can swim
And men can fish
And all have a good time.

Edward Lewis (11)
Abbey Gate College, Chester

Raindrops From Heaven

The raindrop fell through the sky,
On its way it hit a fly.
It bounced into a stream,
Slowly as if in a dream.

A raindrop felt very small,
As it fell into a waterfall.
White rapids froth and foam,
The river goes to the sea, its home.

A raindrop fell from above,
It landed softly like a dove,
It was washed down a drain
And was never seen again.

A raindrop fell into the sea,
Where fishes swim free
And whales and dolphins play,
Whilst ships pass on their way.

Raindrops fall and make a rainbow,
Down on Earth rivers flow.
Rain falls down to feed the land,
Without the rain it turns to sand.

Victoria Cavill (12)
Abbey Gate College, Chester

The Ferry

I stood there waiting in the wind,
feeling cold but thrilled,
that the Dutch lady would take me
from one side of the river to the other.

As she started to dock,
everyone waiting started to shuffle a lot.
Moving forwards to climb on-board,
to race ahead to get the best spot.

On the top my auntie and I
sat huddled together, laughing a lot.
Everyone else was struggling to hold onto their hats
and were tightening their scarves.

The first stop was Seacombe,
people rushed off as others rushed on.
Some beating the raising of the drawbridge,
others not.

We travelled across the river, the next stop was Birkenhead.
At last we were there, feet on solid ground.
No longer did the wind blow in our faces,
as we looked back to say farewell to the Dutch Lady.

Olivia Archer-Jones (11)
Abbey Gate College, Chester

The Howling

It was last night I went to my room,
But I didn't know it was a full moon,
The wind was blowing hard
And the roads white with mist.
Suddenly I got a pain in my wrist,
My body was stretching.
I started growling
And the next minute I was desperately howling.
I bashed down the door in a mad sort of rage.
Running fast down the hard, cold street,
With a supernatural sort of heartbeat.
I roared out loud, horrible and scary.
Then I saw my friend passing by.
I couldn't help myself, and said goodbye.
The noise of sirens rang in my ear.
Next paramedics and police came.
It was obvious I was to blame.
They all looked at my towering shape,
My fur like wire wrapped round me like a long grey cape.
An officer shot,
The silver bullet went flying
And when it hit me they thought I was dying.
My fur dropped off,
The rage was beginning to fade.
Then the police saw I was a boy, lost and afraid.
The anger had stopped,
No more growling
And that was the end of my moonlit howling.

David Kelly (11)
Abbey Gate College, Chester

At The Match

I arrive at the stadium
It's an hour before kick-off
Already the atmosphere is electric
I can see a sea of coloured football shirts
I can feel the anticipation between the fans

Kick-off
A huge roar goes up around the stadium
Beating hearts all around me
The midfielder's lost the ball
Could be a breakaway here!
Good control by the striker
Panic all around!
Oh, it's just wide!
A sigh of relief by the home fans
A goal kick
Up to the striker
Control on the chest
He turns
Shoots . . .
Scores!
As the home fans cheer, the away fans jeer
1-0
The final whistle blows
I leave the stadium full of joy
Now it's . . . next match ahoy!

Joe Bate (11)
Abbey Gate College, Chester

Bonfire Night

I heard a noise, I saw a light,
It zoomed up high,
Then *bang!* (it gave me a fright),
The light shattered into millions of pieces.

I saw flashes of silver
And emerald and gold.
I stood there mesmerised
And jolly cold.

There was another that spun,
Sending out showers of golden rain
And people were running around with sticks,
Which let off sparks as bright as the sun.

The last one was my favourite,
It shot up so high,
I could barely see it,
Then burst into a million pieces.

But when it died away into the darkness,
It felt like the world was clothed in blackness.

Amy Kite (11)
Abbey Gate College, Chester

November Fire

The bonfire is built and ready to go,
The guy is clothed from head to toe,
Kick-start the flames with a heart-stopping roar,
The local children plead for more,
Out come the fireworks, a loud cheer is heard,
We've rockets and bangers (loudest preferred),
Starbursts and glitter trails crisscross up high,
Faces turned upward to pitch-black night sky,
It's over too soon, but the fire is still burning,
Now toward Christmas our thoughts will be turning.

Jonathan Edge (12)
Altrincham Grammar School for Boys, Altrincham

Wintertime

Walking through winter,
Oh damn, I got a splinter.
I am seeing beautiful leaves of gold,
But yet, I am so cold.

Playing basketball in the yard,
I am playing point guard.
But I keep sneezing,
I wonder why, because it is freezing.

I am just leaving,
Gladly still breathing.
In public I dropped my book,
Everyone there gave me a bad look.

Someone behind me gave me a call,
As I turned around I walked into a wall.
It was my friend, Ben Cohen,
But this is my poem.

Dominic Bates (12)
Altrincham Grammar School for Boys, Altrincham

The Morning

Monday's dawning,
Rain is pouring,
Here comes the start of the week.
Going out to
Go to school, while
Newspapers flap at my feet.

I make my way right through the crowded,
Faces of the day.
Arriving at school bang on time,
Ready to work and play.

Alex Stewart (12)
Altrincham Grammar School for Boys, Altrincham

New York

The hustle and bustle of the world's biggest apple,
Packed full of cars, shops and people,
Yellow taxis full of tourists,
In the hustle and the bustle of the world's biggest apple.

The hustle and bustle of the world's biggest apple,
Corner shops, news stands and florists by the park,
Skyscrapers reaching up to the heavens,
In the hustle and bustle of the world's biggest apple.

The hustle and bustle of the world's biggest apple,
Roads snaking by Central Park,
This is the city that never goes to sleep,
In the hustle and bustle of the world's biggest apple.

The hustle and bustle of the world's biggest apple,
Shopkeepers, secretaries, solicitors and bankers,
Car engines, sirens, chattering pedestrians,
All in your visit to the great New York City.

Alex Barker (12)
Altrincham Grammar School for Boys, Altrincham

The Ridiculous World Of Pontaluhu

Strange it would be if man had no bones
A floppy flat creature with little squashed toes
Queer it would be if a fish ruled the land
There's not many rulers with fins not a hand
Crazy it seems but this is all true
In the ridiculous world of Pontaluhu

But though it's quite baffling you should be aware
For I've heard that the wonders are spreading elsewhere
Perhaps it is here this oddness will strike
When tadpoles become bigger than pike
But during this change should you wish to sue
It's the ridiculous world of Pontaluhu.

David Williams (13)
Altrincham Grammar School for Boys, Altrincham

Sikhism

S ikhism is a religion whose New Year starts on a day called Vaisakhi

I t has eleven Gurus (sons of God) one of these Gurus is the
Holy Book (Guru Granth Sahib Ji) which is the last ever
eternal Guru

K angha (comb), Kishera (pants), Kara (bracelet), Kesh (hair)
and Kirpan (sword) are the Five Ks one has to wear when
one becomes a blessed Sikh

H induism is where the religion originates from

I ndia is where the main temple is, which is priceless because
it is made of gold and marble with diamonds and rubies
on the ceiling

S tories are sung in our hymns, which are sung in Gurmukhi
about the lives of Gurus and their teachings

M any people gather at the Temple for the religious ceremonies
after which free communal food (Guru Ka Langar) is distributed
free of charge because the Gurus did not want us to go
empty-handed and by having the same food, taught us
equality and created a classless society.

Harinder Singh Ranshi (12)
Altrincham Grammar School for Boys, Altrincham

Frozen Landscape

The sky's blue, clear and pinkie-purple, with a golden fireball
blinding your eyes.
The beams of light are sparkling between the gaps of clouds.
The jet stream is fluffy and white.
The fields are frozen and the cows are petrified in the frost.
The white glistening trees stand like frozen statues
under a thin veil of mist.
The bushes are prickly claws like witches' fingernails waiting to crunch.
The motorists decrease their speed in anticipation of the risk
of slippery and icy roads.
In the foreground, the blackbirds stand out against the sky.
A plane glinting in the sunlight is reflecting the bright colours
of the rainbow.

Rajiv Sethi (12)
Altrincham Grammar School for Boys, Altrincham

The Beautiful Game

Football is a beautiful game
A sport with great emotion
The fans, cars, money and fame
Thrill of glory and promotion

The chairman wants good results
He speaks to the manager rudely
There must be clever tactics
To win a game so shrewdly

Are you deaf ref?
That was a foul
By player number ten, Raul

A penalty taken on the pitch
Can result in a fabulous goal
A loud roar from the huge crowd
Will move your very soul.

Andrew Veitch (13)
Altrincham Grammar School for Boys, Altrincham

Hallowe'en

Trick or treating, getting sweets
Have a trick if they don't give you treats
Throwing eggs and running like mad
On Hallowe'en you have an excuse to be bad

Dressing up and putting on masks
Dad's old rags which have seen better pasts
White ghostly sheets with cut-out holes
Vile cakes and slime-filled bowls

Dracula teeth and scary eyes
Tadpole soup and frogs' legs pies
Witches, ghosts, Grim Reapers too
Next Hallowe'en, *now what shall I do?*

Christian Sadler (12)
Altrincham Grammar School for Boys, Altrincham

The Seasons

The coldest season of them all,
Wrap up with our winter wool.
It's not the time of year for playing ball,
Cold weather makes it dull.

The season of the newborn,
Newborn cows, lambs, horses and goats.
The seeds produce a new green lawn,
But you still need to keep out the coats.

The hottest season of them all,
Temperatures rise, put the coats away,
Time to play summer sports, these especially with a ball,
We go on the beach where we play.

Time for harvest has come,
The clocks going back an hour.
The start of hibernation for some,
Strong winds cause many leaf showers.

Robert Peters (12)
Altrincham Grammar School for Boys, Altrincham

The Jungle

Dense green undergrowth tangles your feet,
Moist air catches in your throat,
You never know what you might meet,
Here you'll not have time to dote.

A flicker of green, a flash of red,
You start to panic and lose your breath,
A guttural hissing rings through your head
And then you start to think of death.

Philip Conti-Ramsden (12)
Altrincham Grammar School for Boys, Altrincham

Holiday Haikus

Christmas
Christmas is good fun
Eating turkey and pudding
Opening presents

Hallowe'en
Scary Hallowe'en
Collecting delicious sweets
But very spooky

Half term
Yay! Half term is here!
Playing out with my best friends
No more school! Hooray!

Birthday
Another year gone
Party with all of my friends
Happy birthday, Jack!

Jack Sleath (11)
Altrincham Grammar School for Boys, Altrincham

Bonfire Night

Crackle, crackle, crackle,
Goes the bonfire burning bright,
Whoosh, bang, whoosh, bang, whoosh, bang
Go the fireworks in the night,
Pretty colours all around,
Flying in the sky,
Eventually they die away,
Goodbye fireworks, goodbye.

Andar Barrishi (12)
Altrincham Grammar School for Boys, Altrincham

Winter

A blanket of whiteness grips the land,
Marauding snowflakes make their stand.
They flutter down from frosty air,
Their wondrous patterns make people stare.

Snowballs flying through the air,
Thudding happily to a child's chest.
All around are squeals of laughter,
Filling the world with joy and zest.

Hail thundering against the window,
While inside a fire kindles.
Presents torn open, gifts unwrapped,
Christmas Day is here at last.

Gradually snow drips down the wall,
Long gone the coming of Santa Claus.
The sun's hot beams spark up a new thing,
The long awaited coming of spring.

Matthew Furness (11)
Altrincham Grammar School for Boys, Altrincham

Home And Glory

Slowly the ball dropped
Onto the wet, damp grass
The boot hit the ball
Rapidly it moved
Into the air
Going faster and faster
The ball went over the posts
Quickly the crowd
Went wild!

Matthew Smith (11)
Altrincham Grammar School for Boys, Altrincham

My Last Day

M orning came, the sun was high
Y et in my heart I felt I could cry

L ast day of primary school, what a big step
A t last the final target had been met
S aying goodbye to all that I know
T hat day I wished would never ever go

D om, Jade, CJ and Kris
A ll of these friends I'll truly miss
Y esterday I thought of these people
    and in my eyes, tears started to trickle.

Gurdev Ryan Singh (11)
Altrincham Grammar School for Boys, Altrincham

Life

Life is torture, life is pain
Life is wind, life is rain
Life is emotion, life is change
Life is weird, life is strange
Life is great, life is fun
Life is heat, life is sun
Life is kind, life is mean
Life is messy, life is clean
Life is hot, life is cold
Life has problems we need to solve
Life is crazy, life is sane
Life is loss, life is gain
Life is cruel, life is cool
Life is chocolate, life is gruel
Life is young, life is old
Life is stone, life is gold.

Alex Cusick (13)
Altrincham Grammar School for Boys, Altrincham

A Family Holiday

On the 7th August '93,
The Smith family went to Italy,
They went so far, in a rented car,
Then they got on a boat to Sicily.

On a sandy beach they played,
Whilst above them palm trees swayed,
They drove through the town, whilst the sun blazed down,
The children moaned and tempers frayed.

So finally it was time to go home
And it was the parents' turn to moan,
They didn't get on the plane because it was delayed again,
So they took the ship all the way home.

Jamie Taylor (12)
Altrincham Grammar School for Boys, Altrincham

The Fight

At the end of the day
the night is just beginning.
I should get to bed
before my head starts spinning.
I can't quit now,
I'm only now just winning.
I want to go to bed
but my body just isn't quitting.

To fight until the end,
the fight that's just beginning.
This fight, it has no end
and only one beginning.
The fight I fight forever,
the fight I'm always winning.
The fight I want to end,
but the fight is just beginning.

Thomas Paul (11)
Altrincham Grammar School for Boys, Altrincham

Seasons

Drip drop, drip drop
I see the rain pound the ground
People running in distress
Sheltering from the merciless rain

The sun breaks through the shouldering clouds
Bullying its way through the sky
Shedding light where there is none
Bringing heat as it comes

Children come out to play
Stepping out on the wet dew
They stare out to the sky
Searching for a rainbow

The trees drop their precious leaves
Making them bare and ugly
The winds sweep them away
Overtaking everything in its way

The wind brings with it autumn chill
People barely recognisable
Hiding from the cold
The dark fast approaches . . .

The children snuggle up in bed
Protected from the cold
Which never sleeps
And never stops.

Hedayat Javidi (13)
Altrincham Grammar School for Boys, Altrincham

Standing On The Plateau

They stand on the plateau,
Waiting,
Before them, a great chasm,
Over the chasm, another plateau,
On the plateau, more people,
Waiting.
Young and old,
Men and women,
Sitting and standing,
Waiting,
Waiting,
Waiting,
Then they hear it,
Clunk, clunk, clunk.
They freeze and listen.
Clunk, clunk, clunk.
It is coming.
Clunk, clunk, clunk.
The beast appears.
Clunk, clunk, clunk.
It stops between the plateaus,
The people all surge forward,
They reach the waiting beast
And get on the train.

Oliver Marsh (13)
Altrincham Grammar School for Boys, Altrincham

Winter

Winter is the time of year,
When the sky is dull and never clear,
The birds rarely sing outside,
You can't see them float or fly.

Winter is the time of year,
When snow falls down like frozen tears,
Where children have big snowball fights,
In the black darkness of the night.

Winter is the time of year,
When snowy forests are packed with deer,
Eating frozen blades of grass,
Thinking, *will this ever pass?*

Winter is the time of year,
When men should relax and drink some beer,
Sitting down next to the fire,
Chilling out until they tire.

George Flint (11)
Altrincham Grammar School for Boys, Altrincham

Hallowe'en

Zombies ripping out of their graves
Sweets are being eaten rapidly
Vampires stepping out of their coffins
Hallowe'en is a time for fun
So come and trick or treat with me

Ghosts are scaring everyone away
So come and scare with me
You better go trick or treating tonight
Or you'll be dealing with me.

Patrick Tarbuck (11)
Altrincham Grammar School for Boys, Altrincham

Mobile Phone

I'm on the train coming home,
Thinking about a new phone,
Then we slow down and stop,
What a shock!

The train man shouted aloud,
'A bridge has been hit by a lightning cloud.'

'Oh no,' someone gasped.
Then an old man rasped,
'I need a smoke, I'll be quick.'
'Make sure you're back in a tick.'

Oh no, I thought, *how will I let my mum know*?
I had to tell her the train was slow.
If only I had a mobile phone,
I might not feel so alone . . .

Christopher Graham (11)
Altrincham Grammar School for Boys, Altrincham

What Will I Be?

Would I be an astronaut
soaring through outer space
or would I be a race car driver
storming through the race?

Would I be a pilot
working for the air force
or would I be an architect
riding in a Porsche?

All the things that
I could possibly be
which one would that be?

Would I be a builder
building with most of the bricks
or would I be a pop star
singing all the lyrics?

Akshay Chuni (11)
Altrincham Grammar School for Boys, Altrincham

The Song Of Winter

The crisp snow of winter
Crumbles beneath my feet,
This beautiful, glimmering, white snow of winter
Will soon turn into sleet,
I see a robin of winter
With its chest up high and proud,
I watch it hop hungrily
Looking for food upon the ground,
I walk into the garden,
Slipping on the icy floor,
I realise that this will all soon melt,
When spring brings out its thaw,
I walk into the garden to have a look around,
I did not know how bitter cold it was,
While the snow is falling down,
I see gleaming icicles of winter,
Hanging off a branch above,
I feel how bitter cold it is,
So I put on my hat and gloves,
In the winter season,
There is so much to do and see,
So step into your garden
And enjoy it just like me.

Chad Brame (12)
Altrincham Grammar School for Boys, Altrincham

Dragons

Dragons are mythical creatures
Or so some people say,
However I'm pretty sure I saw one,
Just the other day.

I was walking down the high street,
On my way home,
When suddenly I caught a glimpse
Of teeth and wings and bone.

I'm sure it was a dragon,
Though I've not seen one before,
It looked just like a dragon,
Though I never heard it roar.

Big and red and scaly,
With huge, enormous wings,
Eyes like deep blue sapphires
And other scary things!

I blinked and then he vanished
And no one seemed to care,
But when I got to my door,
A red scale was lying there.

I keep it in my bedroom
And look at it at night,
It reminds me of that strange day
I got a dreadful fright!

Vincenzo Cara (11)
Altrincham Grammar School for Boys, Altrincham

The Biggest Bird

It stutters as it starts
And operates the flying parts
The seatbelt signs illuminate
As the rubber wheels begin their pace
The screech of the friction
The sound of the wind gliding past the solid steel wing
The flaps stretch out to their full extent
To lift the creature as they were meant
Its pointed beak drives into the sky
As its large engine gives a loud sigh
The clouds race past as it roars through the air
While all the eyes just blink and stare
It swoops past towns and over the sea
It disturbs the passengers as they slurp their tea
There is no bang and no boom, just a slight hum
Before the rain goes drum, drum, drum
A black cloud appears
As all of the people begin their jeers
The magnificent beast shudders and shakes
That stops the little ones all nice and warm
To open their eyes to scream and bawl
Suddenly the sun appears
So everyone shouts tons of cheers
The bird lands with a sudden bump
That causes all the people to bounce and jump
And so the journey ends, only to start.

Jonathan Birchall (11)
Altrincham Grammar School for Boys, Altrincham

The Gardener

The gardener lived
At the bottom of his shed
And there he made his bed
He said one day that his rabbit flew away
And no one had anything to say

He was very keen in saying this
Although he was very lumpish
He was trying very hard
And with all his might
He did not give up without a fight

He looked very scared and worried
That if he died he might not be buried
And left to lay wherever he may
In the garden shed, the vegetable patch
And the rose bed to decay

But not to worry as there is no hurry
Eighty-nine is no age to part
Many years to go and reap and sow
To dig and weed in the sun and snow
Happily gardening wherever he goes

He's now gone, been a long time dead
Resting in peace in his favourite bed of roses
Daffodils and vegetables galore
Sometimes if you stand and be quiet
You may hear him whistle and the odd snore.

Aszek Assaf (12)
Altrincham Grammar School for Boys, Altrincham

Rajma

(An Indian dish made with kidney beans)

Rajma! Rajma!
You're wonderful
I love you rajma
I can't get enough
You're covered with sauce
And you're sprinkled with cheese
Rajma! Rajma!
Oh give me some more please

Rajma! Rajma!
Piled high in a mound
You slish, you slosh
You stodge around
There's slurpy rajma
All over my plate
Rajma! Rajma!
I think you are great

Rajma! Rajma!
I love you a lot
You're slimy, you're greasy
Delicious and hot
I gobble you down
Oh, I can't get enough
Rajma! Rajma!
You're wonderful stuff.

Aseem Mishra (11)
Altrincham Grammar School for Boys, Altrincham

Arsenal Vs Manchester United

Bust-ups, scuffles
Goals and cards
Passes and penalties
Arsenal Vs United
What a game

Vieira, Keane
Cards all around
Rooney, Campbell
Goals suspected
60,000 fans roaring aloud

Ronaldo, Cole
Watch for the step-overs
Henry, Ferdinand
Titanic clash
Ljungberg, Heinze
The new Argie's game

Fans roaring, *'United!'*
The Gooners screaming
'Vieira . . . whoa!'
Full time is here
And United have *won!*

Ben Askew (11)
Altrincham Grammar School for Boys, Altrincham

The Cliffhanger

There is a strange white house on the edge of Cliff My-Chree,
It has stood there for many a year.
Battered and bruised by the old Scottish weather,
No one has ever ventured inside the house,
People are worried for the old man who lives in the eerie house,
He is said to have been spotted staring at the ships going
                                     by on the misty sea.
Now Cliff My-Chree is about to crumble to the sea's mercy,
It has been threatening to do so for many years,
This old man doesn't seem worried,
He can sense something,
Something dangerous, something frightening, something is coming . .
.

But what? I have that information,
The old man told me,
It's a storm,
A storm is coming.

Sanjay Cain (11)
Altrincham Grammar School for Boys, Altrincham

Bonfire Night Dreams

Raging like a stormy sea of gold,
Towering high up to the stars of night,
Embers glowing in their many
And still the bonfire burns!

Whizzing over land and sea,
Showering sparks rain to the dewy floor below,
No hope, no cares as they crash to oblivion,
But still the fireworks dazzle!

Candyfloss melts on sticky tongues,
As smoke trails slither upwards to the pockmarked sky,
In the shadows the scent of hot dogs hide,
As still the show goes on!

Oliver Tobin (12)
Altrincham Grammar School for Boys, Altrincham

In The Jungle

In the jungle lives Stephen the silly snake
He lives in the trees that are green
When he was born he had a green tongue
But in the trees, now he is never seen

In the jungle lives Larry the laughing lion
He lives in the dead bushes that are brown
When he was born he had a brown tail
But now he lives in the nearest town

In the jungle lives Peter the praying parrot
He lives in the plants that are yellow
When he was born he was red and blue
But you never see him unless you bellow, 'Hello!'

In the jungle lives all my friends
They live in the multicoloured jungle
When they were born they all had something special
But they're my friends because they were born in the jungle.

Christopher Axon (11)
Altrincham Grammar School for Boys, Altrincham

September 11th

On a day three years in the past,
In a dilemma that was so vast,
In a huge city in the USA,
There was a disaster on its way.

As a plane flew overhead,
The next second a building was red,
In the explosion I heard my mum scream,
Which made me drop my ice cream.

9/11 is how it is now known,
The terrorists' hearts must have been made of stone,
I can still hear the screams in my head,
As I'm lying down in my bed.

Benjamin Brayzier (11)
Altrincham Grammar School for Boys, Altrincham

Evil Darkness

The light is fading away . . .
It has finally died.
Died! Died! Died!

In the darkness everything is . . .
Scary, horrible and evil,
Evil! Evil! Evil!

Everything becomes terrifying and alive . . .
Trees are skeletons and cars are ghosts.
Ghosts! Ghosts! Ghosts!

The moon becomes a mournful light . . .
Making ghastly shadows haunt you.
Haunt! Haunt! Haunt!

Midnight is approaching, the clock reads 12 . . .
The night has just begun its horror.
Horror! Horror! Horror!

Vampires attack from behind . . .
Biting until you seep with blood.
Blood! Blood! Blood!

Zombies wander to find more victims . . .
So they can eat their brains.
Brains! Brains! Brains!

The morning has come . . .
To end the evil darkness.
Darkness! Darkness! Darkness!

Joe Bodden-Glennon (12)
Altrincham Grammar School for Boys, Altrincham

Colours

Red!
Red means danger.
Red is the colour of a postbox.
Red is the colour of Man United's kit.
Red is my favourite colour.
This colour is a sign of bad things.
This is what red means to me.

Blue!
Blue is the colour of the swaying of the gentle waves.
Blue is the colour of an extremely hot flame.
Blue is the colour of the sea that stretches to the horizon.
Blue is the colour of the sky way up high.
This colour is a sign of peace and harmony.
This is what blue means to me.

Green!
Green is the colour of tall evergreen trees.
Green is the colour of the long grass in meadows far away.
Green is the colour of an apple up a tree.
Green is the colour of a slimy frog from a green pond.
This colour is a sign of nature and the environment.
This is what green means to me.

Some colours can be good, others can be bad.
Some colours can be lively, some can be calm.
Some colours mean stop and some mean go.
Some colours are special to different people.
Colours can mean all different things
And that is what colours mean to me.

Michael Thurm (12)
Altrincham Grammar School for Boys, Altrincham

What Sport?

As I ran with the ball, the mud slowed me down,
I passed to a player who played for my town.
The other team turned it over and went for a kick,
It hit me right in the stomach and made me feel sick,
What sport am I playing?

As he hit the ball dead straight in the air,
I ran towards it like I just couldn't care.
I positioned myself directly beneath,
I caught out the Sri Lankan much to his grief,
What sport am I playing?

Step-over, step-over, ripping everyone,
Sprinting past all of them, tackled by no one.
I struck the ball with a mighty hit,
The keeper saved it with his giant mitt,
What sport am I playing?

Tom Lloyd (11)
Altrincham Grammar School for Boys, Altrincham

Poems

Poems,
It's always hard to make them rhyme
And get them finished and handed in on time.
Poems,
It's always hard to think of what to write,
Teachers say it's easy, they're not right,
Poems.

Robert Avery (12)
Altrincham Grammar School for Boys, Altrincham

Tornado

Finally it has come,
Has as much damage as a bomb,
Should we hide in fear
Or stay and take a dare?
Should we run
And let the damage be done?
The village is clear,
The twisting and turning we could hear,
Nobody to save us,
Not even our so-called boss,
Here we are hiding,
While away we could be riding,
But it is too late,
It has finally hit the date,
Why didn't we listen?
Then this mess we wouldn't be in,
We are hiding in our den,
No friends, all dead, even our best friend Ben,
Now we fear for our lives,
All the men are dead, even their wives,
Coming closer the din,
Should we just give in?
Our mother and father dead,
Killed on holiday by the same monstrous beast in their bed,
Now we look like rats
And live like bats,
Only coming out at night,
Always having a fight,
Here we are sister and brother,
We might have to say goodbye to each other.

Temidayo Kashimawo (11)
Altrincham Grammar School for Boys, Altrincham

Mr Guy Fawkes!

Guy Fawkes was burned after Hallowe'en,
That night when the demons rise.
On this day, fireworks fly,
Into the dark black sky.
The flames shoot up while people are silent,
Thinking about that human phoenix.
It has a tail like fiery flowers
And a mouth like burning showers.
Can you guess this autumn day
After Hallowe'en and before Christmas Eve?
Yes, you've guessed it,
It's the 5th November, remember, remember.

Thomas Payne (11)
Altrincham Grammar School for Boys, Altrincham

Jazz

Playing this music
Makes me feel alive
Playing this music
Makes me want to jive

Playing the sax
Rhythm and blues
Playing the sax
You can't lose

Playing cool jazz
Making people dance
Playing cool jazz
Making people prance

Putting it away
Fills me with sorrow
Putting it away
I'll play it tomorrow.

Matthew Barry (11)
Altrincham Grammar School for Boys, Altrincham

Guy Fawkes

The night is a witch's cloak wrapped around the Earth
It's funny where we got Bonfire Night from
Guy Fawkes gave its birth
He had a plot, a fearsome plan
To take down Parliament
He'd blow them up with gunpowder
Then run away in a shot
Instead he was caught
So no battle was fought
He was tortured and sent to die
We remember now, by looking in the sky
At the fireworks passing by.

Will Heatley (11)
Altrincham Grammar School for Boys, Altrincham

Bark At The Bonfire

Oh my, oh no, oh dear,
I have to face it every year.
Oh I hate to remember,
The dreaded, awful 5th November.

The flashing fireworks in the sky,
In the shape of a demon eye.
The poor old fellow stuck on the fire,
One of the things I wouldn't desire.

I get myself in such a muddle,
I could end up in a puddle.
With roast beef they try to bribe me,
But I'd rather have some treacle toffee.

So this is what I have to go through every year,
The nerves, palaver, sickness and fear.
I hate getting into a mess,
I'd rather wear a pink, fluffy dress.

Alexander Paterson (11)
Altrincham Grammar School for Boys, Altrincham

Santa Claus

I came downstairs for a drink,
On one Christmas Eve,
When I looked up the chimney
And saw a red sleeve.

I knew it was Santa,
So I helped him down
And I realised, on his face,
He was wearing a frown!

For on this snowy dark
Christmas Eve night,
Something had given Santa
A bit of a fright.

Because Rudolph's nose
Had lost its blaze,
So Santa couldn't
Find his way.

I gave Rudolph a carrot
And his nose became aglow,
Finally Santa rode off
With a merry, 'Ho, ho, ho!'

Billy Kelly (11)
Altrincham Grammar School for Boys, Altrincham

Fireworks

Fireworks make lots of noise,
Eyes stare up at them from girls and boys.

Fireworks are very bright
And light up the damp, cold night.

Old and young love to stare,
At all the colours in the air.

Fireworks screech, bang and frazzle,
Fireworks scream, whoosh and dazzle.

Billy Horner (12)
Altrincham Grammar School for Boys, Altrincham

Where Do All The Teachers Go?

Do they mark our homework?
Are they living on Mars?
Do they ever brush their hair
And do they drive space cars?

Do they ever eat a lot,
Chocolate, ice cream and more?
Do they ever play PC games
And do they get a high score?

Do they ever do any sport,
Running, swimming and football?
Do they ever go to the gym
And do star jumps in the hall?

Do they ever do anything fun
Like watching the TV?
Do they like all the soaps?
Are you sure they're like you and me?

I'll follow one back home today,
I'll find out what they do,
Then I'll put it in a poem,
That they can read to you.

Chris Carruthers (11)
Altrincham Grammar School for Boys, Altrincham

Racing Cars

As they all zoom around the track,
The noise has made the sound barrier crack,
Twisting, turning around the bend,
All battling to get to the end,
As they all cross over the line,
Will they get their record time?
The race is over, the race is done,
Seven were in it, only one won.

Ryan Cunningham (11)
Altrincham Grammar School for Boys, Altrincham

November The Fifth

A November of embers starts tonight
All ablaze with stars alight
Flickering mountains from bonfires
As fireworks go off like shots, *bang!*

It seems just like yesterday
When an evil plot was hatched
By Guy Fawkes and his treacherous gang
To blow up Parliament

But now 'tis but mere child's play
As Catherine wheels fly around
Whizzing, sizzling, flaming tails
Till rainbow pebbles fall

And as the dark blanket of night
Creeps up through the glade
The flames grow thin, darkness reigns
And all shall call it a night

So as I look back at the sky
A night so gloriously spent
I just can't wait three seasons more
To taste sweet ale again!

Tomisin Ashiru (11)
Altrincham Grammar School for Boys, Altrincham

Bonfire Night

Bonfire Night
Happens once a year,
A colourful night,
Which fills animals with fear.

Thousands of fireworks,
Which go as high as Mars,
'Tis as sparkly
As the stars.

From reds to greens,
To blues and yellows,
In the village and town,
To the city and meadows.

From bonfires,
To a burning guy
And the smell of food,
Which you can buy.

When they have finished
And you want to go home,
You walk to your door,
Listening to the oldies moan.

Michael Eyley (11)
Altrincham Grammar School for Boys, Altrincham

Bonfire Night

Oh dear, oh dear
It's that time of year
That night I remember
It's the 5th November
I stand in my house
As quiet as a mouse
But when the fireworks are awoken
My peace will be broken
Then up they all rise
Into the navy blue skies
Up go the fiery petals
Steaming like hot kettles
They're like stars in the autumn dark
All the way above the park
The circles of fire
Keep getting higher and higher
The fiery flowers
Give out burning showers
But now it's started to rain
And there is only golden grain
It falls to the ground
Without making a sound
The people all sigh
And the babies all cry
The smoke has gone down
And the crowd start to frown
The fireworks have gone
Each and every one.

Daniel Pinkerton (11)
Altrincham Grammar School for Boys, Altrincham

The Fifth Of November

Hundreds and hundreds of years ago,
An evil plan started to grow.
Guy Fawkes and his gang,
Wanted to use an enormous bang.

They tried to commit a serious act,
That for sure is a fact.
Later on you will see,
They wanted to kill the monarchy.

They'd stock up on explosives,
Just to fulfil their motives,
Every day they'd get more
And add it to their vital store.

But when it came to the crunch,
They certainly were an awful bunch,
In the end their plan was foiled,
All their hopes had been spoiled,
Because they couldn't kill the royals.

As I told you, now you'll see,
How it all came to be.
The guard heard the sound get louder,
With the sizzle of gunpowder.

And then it was him that got killed,
Down to the ground his blood spilled,
But now we celebrate this tragic day,
With bonfires and fireworks, a wonderful array.

Ryan Al-Hakim (11)
Altrincham Grammar School for Boys, Altrincham

November 5th

Fireworks right through the night
Red, blue, orange and even white
Showering colours falling like rain
Sometimes looking like golden grain
Fiery petals, burning showers, flaming tails
All showing how Guy Fawkes miserably failed
What was he thinking in his jumbled-up brain?
Now every year he feels the pain
Light and flashing colourful showers
Coming to watch are children and others
But there can be danger, keep well back
Don't be scared! Just come for a snack
Watch him burn
Watch him blaze
He's turning black
But he'll be back.

David Roberts (11)
Altrincham Grammar School for Boys, Altrincham

The Guy

As the Catherine wheels are turning,
I'm sitting on the bonfire and my legs are burning.
On top of this dazzling tower of light,
I can see the whole world's plight.

I had an unstoppable plan,
To turn all of England Catholic again,
But alas it did not work
And after that I went berserk.

I was hung and quartered all day long,
The terrible people even cut off my tongue.
So here I am, like a scarecrow,
On top of this fire at a firework show.

Thomas Wells (11)
Altrincham Grammar School for Boys, Altrincham

Night Of Frights

Oh no, it's here again,
I just can't get it out of my brain.
I see those things fly in the air,
That's the thing I just can't bear.

Any minute they will arrive,
Park the car up the drive.
Toffee apples they will scoff,
Whilst setting those horrible fireworks off.

I'm stuck in the kitchen in the dark,
Snap, crackle, bang, it makes me bark.
I see the fire with its flames up high,
I don't like it, it makes me cry.

The noise and sparks have calmed down,
Now I don't have to frown.
All the people start to leave,
Phew, yes, that's a relief.

Christopher Murray (12)
Altrincham Grammar School for Boys, Altrincham

Bonfire Night

As the night grows darker,
The bonfire still not lit,
Guy is tied to a post,
Fixed in a shallow pit!

The noises they make like bang and fizz,
A bursting pop, a squealing whizz,
Fireworks shoot up like burning flowers,
Then fall down in fiery showers!

Catherine wheels spin round and round,
While Guy Fawkes burns to the ground,
The fire is dying, the fireworks are out,
The people are going, there's no one about!

Martin Hawes (11)
Altrincham Grammar School for Boys, Altrincham

The War

The war is a place of chaos
Planes are flying by
Another hand grenade blows up
Blocking out the sky

The enemy drops nightly bombs
Blowing us to bits
The only safe places it seems
Are the sewer pits

The food shortage is getting bad
Shops are running out
Rations are getting worse and worse
What will end this drought?

If we defeat the enemy
Shoot their last balloon
Then we'll be free of fighting
Please let that be soon.

Adam Laycock (11)
Altrincham Grammar School for Boys, Altrincham

Penny For The Guy

Leaves falling, people calling,
Bonfire Night is on the way,
Hallowe'en has come and gone,
Remaining pumpkins light the night,
Bang! Crash! Kaboom!
A firework gives me quite a fright!
I smell the smell of smouldered twigs,
A sight of flashing, whizzing lights,
Different kinds of fireworks, Catherine wheels
And sizzling sparklers are seen throughout the darkness,
As the fireworks begin to die,
I leave for home, penny for the guy?

Sam Cook (11)
Altrincham Grammar School for Boys, Altrincham

Bonfire

The fire is lit and it is spreading higher,
burning leaves, twigs and an old rubber tyre.
This chance only comes once a year,
but cats and dogs still shake with fear.

It is the end of night, but the sky is light,
being illuminated by flashing fireworks, red, blue and white,
Oohs and aahs came from the crowd,
as smoke floated up in one big cloud.

It had ended and Guy Fawkes lay,
crumpled beneath the bonfire display.
I cannot wait until next year,
as the cats and dogs are freed of fear.

Nicholas Johnston (12)
Altrincham Grammar School for Boys, Altrincham

Bonfire Night

My string sizzled
Getting closer and closer
Sparklers fizzled
Getting dimmer and dimmer
Thinking about
What I could be
A streamer?
Maybe a spout
Or I could be a screamer?
Hotter I get
The pressure is building up
I am a jet
The string is short, I will fly
I shoot to the sky
As beautiful as a rainbow
The fans give a sigh
As I fade into the night sky.

Luke Glover (12)
Altrincham Grammar School for Boys, Altrincham

Bonfire Mayhem

As the flame gave a shiver,
The people they quiver.
The rockets go *boom!*
In the light of the moon.
Catherine wheels twirl
And frazzle and whirl.
The guy it is burning,
The soup it is churning.
The spectators are waiting
For the grand finale,
The rockets were great,
But the soup tasted like barley.
As the crowds made their way home,
With happy faces,
They got to their houses,
The kids play races.
They'd run and jump,
Shouting, 'I've won, I've won!'
Then argue and squabble,
The fight had begun.
There was punching and pushing,
Then a drunken dad would say,
'Go on hit him,
He's won, hooray!'
Then Mum came up moaning,
'I knew you'd get hurt!
Look at him crying,
His face is covered in dirt!
You're grounded you two, now go to bed!'
'But what's for tea, Mum?'
'Water and bread!'

Joe Callaghan (11)
Altrincham Grammar School for Boys, Altrincham

Don't Blame The Fire

Why does everyone blame the fire?
But humans are just plain liars,
They choose to use us,
But mostly abuse us.

Guy Fawkes blew up the tower,
Then came a deadly shower
Of fire burning, blazing, killing,
That human is so silly.

Fireworks I hear one night,
Those colours are so bright,
Roman candles is what they use,
But they need fire to light the fuse.

They make noises on Bonfire Night,
Oh what a beautiful sight,
Snap, crackle, pop, bang,
Fire plays an essential part.

Suppose the fire would go away,
No fireworks on bonfire day,
November 5th, no special day,
Let's hope the fire can find a way.

Rory Woodward (11)
Altrincham Grammar School for Boys, Altrincham

Fireworks Flashing - Haikus

Fireworks are flashing
Fiery petals are burning
Bonfires exploding

A human phoenix
The person's pain of the past
The fingers of flame

Roasted marshmallows
Terrific toffee apples
Delicious candy.

Yousaf Ibrahim (11)
Altrincham Grammar School for Boys, Altrincham

Bonfire Night

Oh fire, fire,
You are so bright,
My eyes are burning from your dazzling light.

I can see the sparks in the air,
To be right near one,
I wouldn't dare.

Some of them are glittering golden grain,
Which is falling like the rain,
To miss it all you would be insane.

Now everyone is going home,
I am standing here all alone,
Looks like I'll have to wait until next year,
Night Guy Fawkes.

Jack Hartley (12)
Altrincham Grammar School for Boys, Altrincham

Bonfire

Bonfire, bonfire burning bright
Shining on all through the night
It's a brilliant tower of light
It's a thing of beauty and might

Flashes, bangs all around
Flying around making sound
Little lights spin around
On that night that is renowned

Colours almost everywhere
Giving many pets a scare
The lights look like a flare
The sounds come from here and there.

Liam Townsend (11)
Altrincham Grammar School for Boys, Altrincham

Monster Lizard Found On Road!

There was a lizard in Birkdale,
Found by the side of the road,
It was about two feet long
And had the same skin as a toad.

Found by two lorry drivers,
By the name of Karl and Dave,
They were heading home from work
And found the lizard in a bit of a daze.

Karl and Dave caught the lizard
And took it up to New Cut Lane,
When they showed the shelter manager,
The lizard was in some pain.

The two men then found with quite a shock,
That lizard they found by the side of the road,
Grew to the same size as a bargepole from bottom to top.

Lauren Wilkinson (13)
Burscough Priory Science College, Burscough

Destruction And Devastation

Bush and Blair are in alliance,
Saddam Hussein is in defiance.
The weapons of mass destruction are not here to stay,
So don't be afraid, we'll take them away.

All the people are dying,
The women and children are crying,
The bombs are hitting ground floor
And exploding on their door.

It will all be over soon,
Well, that's what they think,
But when they turn their backs,
All they hear is *boom!*

Cameron McFarlane (12)
Burscough Priory Science College, Burscough

On The Field

The fielders leave the pavilion,
Out on the field they go,
The field is set,
The captains met,
The toss is won,
The toss is lost,
Out on the square,
Where the grass is bare.

The batsmen are ready,
The umpire says play,
The bowler runs in,
On this bright, sunny day,
Off stump, middle or leg with seam,
Off breaker, leg breaker, don't get creamed,
Out on the square,
Where the grass is bare.

The batsman is thinking,
With some luck,
Not out for a duck,
On drive, off drive, cut or pull,
Over the bowler's head, flash or dull,
The ball is fired down,
A leg breaker disguised,
A late cut for the batsman,
Over the rope, he can't believe his eyes,
Out on the square,
Where the grass is bare.

The bowler tries again
And a reward for his persistence,
Through bat and pad,
Seamed with no resistance,
The bails go flying,
It's the end of play,
For both of the teams,
An enjoyable day,
Not on the square,
The grass has been spared.

Mark Huyton (12)
Burscough Priory Science College, Burscough

Fox Hunting

The fox, he kills,
Just to survive,
He's cute and furry
And should stay alive.
The huntsman,
He kills for sport,
Of the pain and suffering,
He has no thought.

The RSPCA are trying their best,
To ban fox hunting forever
And they try to help all the rest,
Even the ones that are killed for leather.

The Queen, she goes hunting,
Yet the R stands for Royal,
Huntsmen, horses and dogs,
Racing through the soil.

The huntsman, just out to kill,
The fox still running fast,
Run, run, the Queen is coming,
How much longer will it last?

Chloe Dorrian (12)
Burscough Priory Science College, Burscough

X-Ray Eyes

One day after watching telly,
I told my mum I could see in her belly.
She said to me, 'Don't tell lies,'
Then she realised I had X-ray eyes.

Word got out that this was true,
People said to me, 'What's wrong with you?
Are you an alien, ghost or witch
Or are you lying to make yourself rich?'

The kids at school took the mick,
But other people asked, 'Are you sick?'
I had to tell them no or yes,
It put me under a lot of stress.

Later on I want to go to medical college,
This will help me increase my knowledge.
Everyone knows now that I never told lies,
I just told them what I saw with my X-ray eyes!

Cathy Ingham (13)
Burscough Priory Science College, Burscough

The Night Man

Once every night,
The night man comes,
He creeps silently through the street,
Like a bird on its prey.
The only light the street has are his eyes,
Like a torch attached to him everywhere he goes,
His breath is like the wind,
Breathing softly in the air.
He knocks on my window,
Like a ghost haunting me!
His fingers are like ice,
Moving everywhere he goes.
He then sits silently,
In a weak, silent pose.

Louise Boardman (12)
Burscough Priory Science College, Burscough

My Friend's Dog!

My friend's dog is a golden retriever,
He's cute and fluffy
And jumps up to meet yer,
When he was small,
He was quiet as a mouse,
But now he's big, he bounds round the house.

He leaves big paw prints on the floor,
But on the front of my T-shirt,
There's even more.

He loves to play football
And is actually quite good,
Though sometimes he gets excited
And starts rolling in the mud.

My friend loves her dog,
She plays with it every day,
My friend loves her dog
And she's trying very hard,
To make Harvey obey!

Bethany Richards (12)
Burscough Priory Science College, Burscough

Rocket Horror!

At 9.10 at night, a family was given a fright,
Bang! Firework, the house was filled with smoke
That gave them a terrible choke.
No one was hurt, just shock to blame, no terrible pain.
The 'exploding horror' came through a letter box,
Caused great criminal damage.
The commercial type bomb that no one knows where it came from,
Gave them a trembler that they will not want to remember.

Stephen Hayter (12)
Burscough Priory Science College, Burscough

Kes

(Inspired by 'Kes' a play adapted from 'A Kestrel for a Knave' by Barry Hines)

Trained to perfection,
Trained to perfection for a year or two
Kes, astonishingly trained . . .
After, 'Kes, come on girl.'
There's a whoosh and a swoop and she's back.

Billy Casper, Billy Casper:
Home life, no good,
School life, no good.
At home, Jud's a pain to him,
Bossing him and bullying him.
At school, MacDowall's a pain to him,
Bossing him and bullying him.
No change there then.

No one understands him,
Him and his imaginary world.
In his world
Billy the Hero with Desperate Dan,
Fighting all evil,
All evil in 'The Dandy',
'The Dandy' comic strip,
Him and his imaginary world.

After games,
Shoved in the shower,
Turned down cold.
Forgets to place the bet for Jud.
Back at school, lessons again,
School bell goes, home again,
Home again, only to find a horrible tragedy,
Kes,
Kes killed.

All Jud's fault, Jud killed Kes.
Billy, Billy, heartbroken Billy.
The only one in Billy's life
Who could make him feel better
And now she's gone,
Billy, Billy, heartbroken Billy.

Georgina Hales (12)
Burscough Priory Science College, Burscough

The War In Iraq

The allied army storm the square,
As the Iraqis fire, they don't care,
But still the armies charge them down,
As comrades on both sides fall to the ground.

Helicopters fall from the sky,
Leaving a trail of black smoke so high,
But then in the distance,
The tanks can be heard,
Ready to crush and turn in a herd.

As soldiers sleep
And families weep,
The battle goes on,
Week after week.

When the end is near,
People's hearts fill with fear.
'Has Saddam been captured?'
They say.

At last it is true,
The battle is won . . .
But the war is not over,
The war is not won.
Some might say it's
Just begun.

Craig Kewley (13)
Burscough Priory Science College, Burscough

Rocket Horror

It was dark, it was quiet on that dreadful night,
The family of three had the most terrible fright,
The rocket from hell thundered into their home,
It whistled and crackled with a deathly moan.

A cloak of darkness wrapped around the house,
After the explosion it was quiet, as quiet as a mouse,
Then screams of panic and shattering glass,
Sparks of flames . . .
Thank God it didn't hit the gas.

Firemen and police were quick on the scene,
Rushing to the rescue they were very keen.
What a disgusting mess they could see,
Why couldn't those thugs let the poor family be?

No one was hurt, it is hard to believe,
On that night of the rocket horror scene,
The rocket's sounds of bangs and booms,
Still haunt them at night when curled up in their rooms.

Alexander Bailey (13)
Burscough Priory Science College, Burscough

Our World!

Clouds billowing against the blue of the sky
Planes leaving vapour trails because they fly so high

Trees and bushes swaying slightly in the breeze
Flowers full of pollen being tended by the bees

The distant cooing of a wild dove calling for a mate
A train goes thundering down the lines, perhaps it's running late

The cry of seagulls in the air as they glide with grace and flare
They really are a lovely sight in their down of grey and white

At this time of the year, there is nothing to compare
Knowing at last that summer's here, not there.

Thomas Virtue (12)
Burscough Priory Science College, Burscough

A Man's Best Friend

Who am I?
I wake and open my big brown eyes
My nose is cold and wet
I stretch out my fluffy body
And wag my tail

I love to play and get some treats
Going for a walk is the best
Along I walk, lead in mouth
I like to swim in the canal
But I hate being washed afterwards
When I'm ill I visit the vet
They make me better
And give me treats

I love to run round and play
I make everyone laugh
Who am I?
I am man's best friend
A dog, of course!

Hannah Griggs (12)
Burscough Priory Science College, Burscough

Argh! The Aliens Are Coming!

There was a young boy called Ted
He always sleeps in his bed

When the aliens are here
It's only screams that you will hear

They are only three feet high
And some only have one eye

As you walk along the hall
Their eyes appear through the wall

Beware all you children in bed
You could be seeing the alien, Ted!

Jessica Waring-Hughes (12)
Burscough Priory Science College, Burscough

My Football Season

I play for Burscough FC,
This was a big thrill for me,
We played lots of matches,
We won a lot,
Then really excited I got.

The league started off,
We were playing well,
We had won all our matches
And scored lots as well.

At the end of the league was the final,
We still hadn't lost a game,
More nerve-racking it couldn't have been,
As Redgate were a good team,
We played well and it was 1-1,
Then in extra time,
I knew it could be,
I went and scored from the halfway line
And saved us all in extra time.

Three nights later we played again,
In another final once again,
They scored,
We scored,
They scored,
They scored,
This was a disaster as you can tell,
We were crying a lot as well,
At least it was quite fun,
We still have a dozen new seasons to come!

Sarah Lygo (13)
Burscough Priory Science College, Burscough

God 911

Who is God?
What does He want?
Does He hide in shame?
Why do we take the blame?

If God was truly real,
Why does He let people steal?
Why do children in Africa die?
Oh please, oh please, tell us why!

And people think that God is fair!
If He is, then He would truly care!
I know people go to church to pray,
For the self-righteous, it's just their way.

They say that God's the great creator,
Not true, you'll see sooner or later.
East Vs west, black Vs white,
Too many deaths, religion's not right.

Peace and tolerance is what we should seek,
But we're not quite ready to be led by the meek,
Too many gods, too many stories,
Each of them claiming the power and the glory.

Don't be mad at me,
You'll see!
Just look back
Through all your history.

Nathan Davies (12)
Burscough Priory Science College, Burscough

Shopping

Watch them tins
Mind your head
When we get home you're going to bed
Leave them cans
They are the man's
Put that back
Or you'll get a smack

Fetch me the cheese
It's not that bad
Now come on and
Don't be like your dad
Sit in this trolley
Keep your fingers inside
Stay out of trouble
And you might get a ride

Now go to the desk
I'm ready to pay
Pass me the beans
And we'll be OK
Put that back
Leave the ice cream
Give me it now
Oh, he's starting to scream

Everyone's looking
At you and me
I'm getting in a fluster
You're embarrassing, *see!*
Quick as we can
Into the car
Let's get home
It's not that far.

Francesca Bailey (12)
Burscough Priory Science College, Burscough

My Baby Brother

Mum and Dad sat me down,
They said they had something to say,
The thing I'd wanted for so long,
There's a baby on the way.

It seemed to take forever,
Those 9 months for baby to grow,
But finally the time had come,
Off to the hospital we go.

I ran into the room,
When I heard a baby cry,
I held him very carefully,
My baby brother had arrived.

And now I can't remember
What life was like before he came,
My darling baby brother
And Alex is his name.

Amy Lea (12)
Burscough Priory Science College, Burscough

9/11

Tall and fine, a stunning skyline,
Shimmering and sleek, a working week,
Hustle and bustle, the papers rustle.

A domestic flight, an unaware plight,
Planes hijack, an infamous attack,
Hijackers in the plane, they were insane.

Planes crashed, everything smashed,
Shocked screams, destroyed dreams,
Dust, fire, smoke, how could people cope?

On Ground Zero there were many heroes,
People's hearts broken apart,
9/11, peace in Heaven.

Tayla Murphy (12)
Burscough Priory Science College, Burscough

Red, The Lurcher

Red, the cheeky dog,
He goes through the midnight fog,
Just to help the friendly dogs in
Battersea Dog's Home.

Bolt, lift and draw,
Like a secret agent,
Creeping, lurching,
Searching
For food in the kitchen.

As he creeps, he lets his friends out
And gives a shout,
'To the kitchen!'
They all run,
They just want fun.

Bolt, lift and draw,
Red, the Lurcher,
Is quite a searcher,
In the past he was starved,
But now he can't get enough
Of the steaks that are so tough!

Rebecca Williams (12)
Burscough Priory Science College, Burscough

Arab The Champion!

Speed, agility, stamina, power,
Fame, popularity,
Close to humanity,
Intelligence, friendliness,
Arab the champion!

Creature unique,
Athletic physique,
Arab ribs number 17,
Other breeds number 18,
Arab the champion!

Harness, dressage, trekking, endurance,
Good-natured and liveliness,
Speed and kindness,
Tall and powerful,
Arab the champion!

Greatest of all domestic breeds,
Other horses cry and plead,
'Help us to be like you,'
Arab the champion!

Katy Taylor (12)
Burscough Priory Science College, Burscough

Final Score 6-2

Giggs nets a goal,
It breaks the keeper's soul,
But there is more to come,
If you didn't know it, you must be dumb,
Rooney nets number 2,
They're on a roll,
Still breaking the keeper's soul.

Rooney nets again
The fans are going insane,
They pull one back,
Just one more goal than Jack,
Hat-trick hero Rooney,
The keeper's getting moody,
Still in possession,
Fenerbache have a lack of concentration,
Sir Alex Ferguson is pleased,
Fenerbache manager can't breathe.

United playing so well,
Fenerbache are as if they are in Hell,
Fenerbache pull another back, 4-2,
Fenerbache running around as if they need the loo.

4-2, 4-2,
Van Nistelrooy spreads it to 5-2,
They are not finished yet,
How much would you bet,
Bellion with the final goal,
Continuously breaking the keeper's soul.

Daniel Bradshaw (12)
Burscough Priory Science College, Burscough

September 11th

Was it a disaster movie? Was it a bad dream?
'Help me, help me,' you could hear people scream.
When terror struck many people were stuck,
On the day of September 11th.

The Towers crashed down to the ground,
The world watched without a sound.
No one could believe the horror seen before them,
On the day of September 11th.

Memories fade but we will never forget
All the people we never met
Millions of tears cried for all those that died
On the day of September 11th.

Hannah Nicholson (13)
Burscough Priory Science College, Burscough

Death Of Dolphins!

The dolphins are so friendly and kind,
But lots of dead dolphins you can find.

The dolphins are dying more and more,
This has to stop for sure,
There needs to be a cure.

The hunters have been beating,
For some of the Japanese it is for eating.

This is for a Japanese delight,
But for the dolphins it is a fright.

The water is full of red blood,
For the dolphins this isn't good.

This killing is so wrong,
This shouldn't have gone on for so long.

Rachel Hesketh (12)
Burscough Priory Science College, Burscough

Unbelievable, Unsinkable

A new ship sails from Liverpool
It's 1912 and America calls
Titanic is the ship of their dreams
Unbelievable, unsinkable
Rich and poor alike
Families, lords, ladies, artists
Sail forth in April
Unbelievable, unsinkable

Fabulous food, ice for the drinks
Cool linen, clean glassware
New friendships give delight
Unbelievable, unsinkable
Relationships forming, dancing all night
Drinking in the ship's pleasures
Unbelievable, unsinkable

The dark of the ocean, the dark of the night
Swirling fast music
A crack! A wrenching sound
Unbelievable, unsinkable
The iceberg extends its arms above
And destiny reaches out below
To the ship of dreams
Unbelievable, unsinkable

Noise, shouts, screams
Anguish, separations from loved ones
Fathers and daughters pulled part
Unbelievable, unsinkable
Ice-cold, freezing cold
Drowning, drowning, no one came back
Fifteen hundred are quiet, still
Unbelievable, unsinkable.

Alice Gradwell (12)
Burscough Priory Science College, Burscough

The Great Fire Of London

In 1666 Pudding Lane
There was a bakery who gained its fame
But the next day there was a disaster
Was it the carelessness of a maid or master?

'Fire, fire!' shouted the maids and masters
Rushing with water faster and faster
It broke out the bakery with a fierce flame
Everybody knew this was no game!

Pigeons dropping to the ground from the sky
There was not a happy sound only scream and cry
People loading their belongings into some boats
Endlessly coughing with sore throats

The malicious flame ate everything in its path
Leaving a very disastrous aftermath
80% of the city was destroyed that night
To build it again it will be a tough fight.

Melissa Bailey (12)
Burscough Priory Science College, Burscough

November Rolled

November rolled into December
The city was freezing at night
With temperatures dropping so suddenly
It gave us all such a fright

We're quite looking forward to spring
When we know that the thaw will begin
So we'll sit by the fire
And be quiet until January comes walking in.

Jessica Dixon (12)
Burscough Priory Science College, Burscough

In Memory Of Baby Samantha

Here she comes,
Here she is,
A beautiful baby girl,
Welcome to the world,
She came out in one big rush,
She came out with one big push,
Into the arms of love.

There she was in the arms of love,
But then she went blue,
What was happening?
No one had a clue,
The baby was snatched from the mother's arms,
All she could hear were the nurses telling her to stay calm.

Test tubes here,
Test tubes there,
There were test tubes everywhere,
In the incubator she lay dying.

Two weeks gone
And no hope,
The mother and father were finding it hard to cope.

They fought and fought for her little life,
Trying and trying to bring her back,
But it was too late,
This was her calling to God's Pearly Gates.

We are all sorry,
She is gone,
She'll be missed.

This is her poem, sealed with a kiss.

Jessica Mooney (12)
Burscough Priory Science College, Burscough

Parker On The Go

Parker here, Parker there, Parker everywhere
The unemployed midfielder is so good
But he looks like he's going to Liverpool hood

The Blues are third in the league
So I think he should leave
He might get them to the Champions League

Now that would be a sight to see
Beating Real Madrid and his old team Chelsea

He's going for 5 million pounds
Now that's cheap for a bag of skills

He will be loved at Everton
With a ton of love

Now to the team

Martyn in net, stopping the goals
Hibbet, Stubbs, Jobo, Naysmith, all in defence,
They will be hard to get past with them Scousers at the back
Now to the midfield
Watson, Gravesen, Parker, Kibane
What a midfield, solid as bricks
Now to the forwards
Cahill and Bent
Scoring goals forever and ever

What a team
To hold up the Premier League
Or maybe the Champions League . . .

Cameron Cox (12)
Burscough Priory Science College, Burscough

Silence

All the children back for their very first day
They've all been off for a nice summer's play
Mothers, fathers and babies too
How could it happen? How could it happen?

Crash!
The doors slam open
And strangers storm in
Bearing guns, they start making a din
People run everywhere and bullets are shot
How could it happen? How could it happen?

1,000 people all squashed in a room
Some of them dead, they've hit their doom
Wires are hung from wall to wall
But these aren't Christmas lights, no! Not at all!
How could it happen? How could it happen?

Day number two, mothers and babies set free
But what about the other child? What about me?
Terrorists getting stricter and people getting ill
How could it happen? How could it happen?

Children are stripped from their waist to their head
All they wanna do is go to sleep in their bed
But that's not right, no that's not safe
Coz the man with the switch is waiting, just waiting

Bang!
Then silence for a minute or two
Then screams from everywhere
Screams, but from who?
Screams of pain
And screams of sorrow
But will they live to see tomorrow?

Arms over here and legs over there
The terrorists are dead, they don't even care
People have been blown from one into two
How could it happen? How could it happen?

Blood-covered people all carried out
No one wants to see them
No one wants to count
The hospitals are full and the school is too
How could it happen? How could it happen?

1,000 people all trapped in that room
Over 300 dead just because of that boom
400 people still haven't got names
Because of those people who were playing a game
This all happened in September 2004
Because of those people who slammed through that door.

Hannah Brocken (12)
Burscough Priory Science College, Burscough

Everton

Rarely do footballers get so lucky on Merseyside,
Could be relegated but we know they will survive.

After one of the best starts in 28 years,
We know we can win something, no more tears.

After selling Wayne Rooney everyone took the mick,
They thought we could do nothing, it makes me feel sick.

With Z Cars booming on match day
And Everton scoring goals, *hooray!*

With Alan Stubbs leading the team out
And David Moyes giving him a shout.

Knowing that we can't lose,
We let the opposition have a snooze.

With The Toffees playing every week,
Do we need the players we seek?

Alex Noon (12)
Burscough Priory Science College, Burscough

Hunger In Sudan

When will the hunger in Sudan stop?
The conflict will have to cease,
Kids stuck, having to work.

When will the hunger in Sudan stop?
Kids are dying,
The conflict must finish.

When will the hunger in Sudan stop?
Oxfam have to send food out to these people,
The rebels must go.

When will the hunger in Sudan stop?
The government in Sudan will have to get rid of the rebels,
The government in Sudan will have to get rid of the rebels.

Sophie Hill (12)
Burscough Priory Science College, Burscough

Football

Football is my favourite sport
And J always plays it
I am certain I will never dismay it,
Even though I am really short!

Lean Osman is the best,
Clearly better than the rest.
Everton are my favourite team,
I'd love to play for them as a dream.

22 players on a pitch,
Passing the ball between them.
Shooting and scoring,
But sometimes missing.

Three different kits,
Everyone must fit.
Three different colours,
But they're not multicoloured.

Teddi Forshaw (13)
Burscough Priory Science College, Burscough

The Beatles

Imagine there were no Beatles,
The 'Yellow Submarine' would be 'Back in the USSR',
'The Blackbird' would fly down 'Penny Lane'.

Walking down the 'Strawberry Fields'
To the beat of Ringo's drum,
'Eleanor Rigby' taking a 'Day Tripper'
Across the Mersey,
'Eight Days a Week'.

John and Yoko took to their bed,
Trying to 'Give Peace a Chance',
George and the Marharishi,
I listen carefully to the solo,
'While My Guitar Gently Weeps'.

Paul and Sgt Pepper walk down
'The Long and Winding Road',
Bought a 'Ticket to Ride'
On 'The Magical Mystery Tour'.

Alexander Cooke (12)
Burscough Priory Science College, Burscough

Eddie The Elephant

Eddie is grey,
Eddie is big,
Eddie doesn't have hair
Or doesn't wear a wig.

Eddie has tusks,
They are white and small,
Eddie has a trunk,
It is very tall.

Eddie is very heavy,
He is the largest land mammal.
He lives in East Africa,
But not in the desert with a camel!

Eddie eats grass
And other solid foods.
Eddie is not the friendliest of animals,
But he doesn't get in a mood.

Hayley Wareing (12)
Burscough Priory Science College, Burscough

Dolphins

The dolphins' last dive,
They were in so much pain,
Until the water ran red,
Only a few minutes until they were dead.

The dolphins' last dive,
There was no way they could survive,
The water ran red,
The dolphins were dead.

The dolphins' last dive,
They were in so much pain,
Why are they doing this?
Shouldn't we complain?

The dolphins' last dive,
Because of these people,
Coastlines run red
And the dolphins are dead.

But why are they doing this?
Why are they killing?
Because animal cruelty goes on,
But soon everything will be gone.

Rachel Bunting (12)
Burscough Priory Science College, Burscough

The Suicide

Courtney Love hired
she was one who was admired
her husband committed suicide
she was getting a divorce
but she cried and cried for her husband who died

Courtney Love said
'Only cowards blow smoke once they're exposed they run and hide'
every single lie was denied about this murder
everyone in the media heard her

Run, run, run
in one room above the garage
he was found
and now no more marriage

He had in fact killed himself
people missed him
it was no laughing matter
no one wished for this to happen
and now everyone's saddened.

Laura Baldwin (13)
Burscough Priory Science College, Burscough

The King Of Fat Cats

There was once a cat,
That was so fat
All it could do was sit on the mat.

The whale with whiskers
Is coming through,
Watch out, wide load!
The king is through.

He weighs 36lbs
And fell down the stairs,
With a belly like that,
He could squash a mouse flat.

Now he is on a diet,
No more sweets,
'Oh please Dad!
Can't I have just one more treat?'

Emily Farley (12)
Burscough Priory Science College, Burscough

Battle Of Britain

(Harry Woods, England 1939-1941)

Airplanes, airplanes, airplanes
All in the blue sky
Guns and bombs are here, there and everywhere
All that you can hear

Crash, crash, bang, bang
Planes are blowing to pieces
Everybody is everywhere
Including me, will I die?

I'm tumbling and twisting widely in the air
I reach for my ripcord as hard as I can
My parachute jerks me up
I'm hanging here like a puppet swinging about

As I am hanging here, shells are whistling past me,
I am hanging here in fright, I am certain I will die,
Maybe my turn has come like the others!

Vanessa Lamb (12)
Burscough Priory Science College, Burscough

A Bus Driver

A bus driver became very poorly
Into hospital he needed to go
The nurses and doctors looked after him
But his survival just wasn't to be so

His wife was very grateful
For the care that he received
She chose to keep his memory alive
Her thoughts of him would never leave

A request for donations instead of flowers
As a big thank you she wanted to buy
A gift of two wheelchairs for hospital use
A great benefit they would apply

The wheelchairs in memory of her husband
The hospital gratefully received
Their use would be a great benefit
Keeping his memory alive, she was relieved.

Oliver Howarth (12)
Burscough Priory Science College, Burscough

Astrology

Astrology, geology, astrology is the best
Gemini and Capricorn
Let's take the test
It's all about stars
Your planet might be Mars

Astrology, geology, astrology is the best
Gemini, Virgo, Leo and all the rest
They are all stars and signs
That people have seen in their minds

What's your future ahead?
What's your sign said?
What does it mean?
What have they seen?

Astrology, geology, astrology is the best
What have they said?
What's your future ahead?

Lauren Kelly (12)
Burscough Priory Science College, Burscough

World War II

Bang! Another bomb dropped as an aircraft went by,
One hundred and fifty people just died,
As panic struck London Town again,
Our quiet family evening was disturbed by the cries.

As enemy planes swooped down low,
Dropping things as they flew,
Destroying towns and cities too,
If only the ARP officers knew.

Sitting in the dead of night,
Make no noise, silent night,
Curtains closed, light excluded,
Not a peep, a sound or movement.

After many attacks, people were mourning,
Lives lost from some big explosions,
Needy hearts and paining children.
World War II was a disastrous event,
Hopefully never to happen in history again.

Jennifer Scully (12)
Burscough Priory Science College, Burscough

Atlantis

Atlantis, an island in the sea,
Looked over by Poseidon with glee,
His first-born son's land you see,
With walls and canals which circle the sea.

Happy are the people here,
Nothing fear,
Live in peace and harmony,
With no need for any money.

Then one day all was lost,
The Earth quaked, oh what a cost,
The waves lashed upon the land,
Nothing was left, not a grain of sand.

But today we think it was once here,
As Plato's fable we love to hear,
Atlantis waits beneath the sea,
For people to find, maybe you, maybe me.

James Seddon (13)
Burscough Priory Science College, Burscough

England Vs Wales

England versus Wales
Many football tales
Some said Wales should have won
England already had it done

When Frank Lampard scored the goal
It hit so hard it could have left a hole
When Frank Lampard scored
All England fans roared

When the second half had begun
Beckham made an excellent run
Took it round one defender
Finished it off with a massive bender

At the end of the lot
Giggs had a chance for an amazing shot
Wales had their chance to have it done
England already had it won.

Sean Howard (12)
Burscough Priory Science College, Burscough

Autumn

The mornings are meeker than they were
The nuts are getting brown
See the autumn bonfires
Sending smoke around the town

I hear the cry of hounds and
Noisy bugles passing by
The thunder of horses' feet
All the hue and cry

Summer is over
Trees are all bare
Mist in the garden
Frost in the air

Winter is coming
And everyone grieves
But isn't it lovely kicking up leaves?

Dale Cheetham (12)
Burscough Priory Science College, Burscough

Mount St Helens

One hundred years ago,
What was formed was a volcano,
It was still where it stood,
Made of stones, rocks and mud,
Inside was red-hot tar.

No life had seen the volcano,
Until about last week or so,
When with all its thirst,
It was ready to burst,
Was the volcano now named St Helens.

After September 11th, everyone felt pain,
After all of the tornadoes and hurricanes,
America is a disaster zone,
Even the people feel accident prone,
Now St Helens might erupt.

Zoe Bober (12)
Burscough Priory Science College, Burscough

Iraq Attack

'Save us, save us,' said someone in cell one,
'Help, help, help!' said someone in cell two,
'Why is this happening?' said someone in cell three,
Why is there all this torture and cruelty?

This is happening because you bombed the Twin Towers,
We must have been digging for hours and hours,
Many were killed when the planes did dive,
That is why this is happening.

Killing, killing, stop the killing,
Death, death, stop the death,
We need help, us and the rest,
Saddam did this, not us!

We are terrified, starving and dying,
Please stop this mass destruction,
Please save us, please, we beg you,
We're scared, please stop this destruction.

Nicole Dawson (13)
Burscough Priory Science College, Burscough

The Death Of Caron Keating

Smiling with laugher, Russ was so proud,
Of his loving and devoting wife, Caron, who shone in a crowd,
Young Caron was a TV presenter for Blue Peter,
She was pretty and there were lots of people who wanted to meet her.

Soon time passed and she retired with two young boys,
She gave them everything they wanted, love, books and toys,
Then Caron grew very ill and battled with cancer,
She still smiled and sang and was a good dancer.

But her husband, Russ, wouldn't tell her she had 18 months to live,
Or she would give in, give up and Russ would never forgive.
So he kept it to himself, years passed by, he was so lucky
that she didn't die,

But they went on a trip to France,
Whilst Charlie and Gabriel rested with Gran,
Russ knew she would have no chance.
So he drove back to Sevenoaks in Kent,
He drove and drove and back they went.

They went back through the roads of Kent,
Through the windy road they went,
They were back in Kent at home,
Where Russ and Caron were alone.

Suddenly Caron gave a smile,
But that only lasted for a while,
Soon she was dead and gone,
But forever in Russ' heart Caron's smile will live on!

Wendy Walker (13)
Burscough Priory Science College, Burscough

Iraq Fights Back

This all happened a few months ago
American and British soldiers say goodbye
Some only teenagers, some older
They charge to Iraq, scared they might
Never see their loved ones again

When they arrive
People flee to homes
Not wanting to die
But to survive
But soldiers still kill thousands of innocent lives
Just to find . . . nothing

A few months down the line
Ken Bigley and two Americans captured
The first one killed
The second one killed, both American
Why?

Ken still alive, his family pleading for his release
Tony Blair doing the best he can
They want people free, then they will let Ken go
So we free one
But is it enough?
What will happen next?

But you have to remember
What started this off
We did this, we have destroyed people's lives
And this is our punishment.

Georgina Richards (12)
Burscough Priory Science College, Burscough

Baghdad Rap

North of Baghdad,
Thousands fled,
North of Baghdad,
Thousands dead.
Rifles on rooftops,
Grenades in streets,
This went on for weeks and weeks.

North of Baghdad,
Beheaded men,
North of Baghdad,
Rebel den.
Ramadi, Falluja and Sadr City,
The poor people there, you would pity.

North of Baghdad,
Unleashed mortars,
North of Baghdad,
American soldiers.
Car bombs by an American convoy,
This was the rebel gangs' evil ploy.

North of Baghdad,
Thousands fled,
North of Baghdad,
Thousands dead.
Forty-one dead,
Plus forty-seven,
All the bystanders up in Heaven.

Samantha Holden (12)
Burscough Priory Science College, Burscough

Ken Bigley

Ken Bigley was a man of 62,
Just one job left to do,
Went to work in Iraq,
Courage he did not lack.

Hour to hour, day to day,
Hope for them never fades away,
Two Americans cruelly slaughtered,
Bigley left to be tortured.

Demands of prisoners to be released,
Bigley's courage never ceased,
Tony Blair can't meet the request,
Doesn't know what is best.

All the world behind this man,
Wishing him all the luck we can,
Bigley now in desperation,
The world prays for his salvation.

The three men would not give in,
They committed a terrible sin,
An innocent man was killed that day,
To Heaven he was whisked away.

Rachel Fenelon (12)
Burscough Priory Science College, Burscough

Rain

Rain, rain, it's been raining for many days
And now because of the rain
There are floods, floods, floods

Floods, floods, floods
People sand-bagging trying to win
If they lose the water will get in
And now because of the rain
There are storms, storms, storms

Storms, storms, storms
Is that all we have these days?
I mean all we ever get is rain
Fire brigade had to use a pump
To pump out the rain
But now the rain has stopped, stopped, stopped

Sun, sun, sun
All we get is sun
The rain has stopped, dried up
We have no rain!

Rebecca Kite (12)
Burscough Priory Science College, Burscough

The Shocking Attack!

Quiet it was that night,
Until Duane started a fight,
He took it outside,
The law he didn't abide,
Until Duane spotted someone else.

He picked up a wine bottle
And with a throttle,
Hit Davies over the head,
At this point he was nearly dead,
But then to come was a second blow,
Smashing the bottle so,
Then Davies was left to die,
Nothing to be seen but a fly.

At the Crown Court,
There was no battle to be fought,
As Duane had pleaded guilty.

Behind bars he was put,
18 months, tut, tut, tut,
To pay for his crime,
There to do his time.

Gemma Knell (12)
Burscough Priory Science College, Burscough

You Killed John Lennon

John Lennon was killed,
By an obsessed fan,
Shot multiple times,
You pulled the trigger Chapman,
You killed John Lennon.

Mark D Chapman,
A very lonely man,
Put in a prison cell,
You pulled the trigger Chapman,
You killed John Lennon.

You were up for parole,
They didn't agree,
You're still in that prison cell,
You pulled the trigger Chapman,
You killed John Lennon.

Chapman shot a legend,
For a moment of fame,
Was it really worth it?
You shot a legend Chapman,
You killed John Lennon.

James Power (12)
Burscough Priory Science College, Burscough

Fireworks

It is late at night
And you are going to bed
When you have got no scary things in your head

Then you hear someone coming to your door
That is when you jump to the floor

Then there's a *bang*
Then there's a *crash*
That's when everything is smashed

You and your family run outside
But you just want to hide

When you look, your house is on fire
All your things, everything you desire

'It's a firework,' people are saying
But who would put it in my home?
It makes my family feel alone

Don't people know what they are doing
Or do they just like to ruin
Things for me and my family?

But now things are better and things are right
But it has made me scared at night!

Aliki Panteli (12)
Burscough Priory Science College, Burscough

Charlotte Wyatt

Little baby Charlotte Wyatt
Lying in your cot so quiet
Your dad waits with you day and night
Tiny hand grips his fingers so tight

The doctors say you can't survive
But your parents want to keep you alive
You came too soon, you'll never walk
Or see or hear or even talk

When you were born, you were five inches long
Weighing one pound, something was wrong
Stopped breathing five times, but still you are here
Your mum thinks about you, always in fear

For eleven months you've refused to die
Not a sound from your lips, not even a cry
You are a fighter, a brave little thing
So much love and joy you could bring.

Emma Binns (12)
Burscough Priory Science College, Burscough

James And The Giant Pumpkin

Nearly autumn,
Nearly autumn,
Local people surprised,
Giant pumpkin competition
Caught their eyes.

Not enough sun and too
Much rain,
The pumpkins won't grow,
What a shame.

They designed a website to
Exchange their seeds,
So they can grow their pumpkins
And keep away weeds.

One lucky person will win
The prize,
For the biggest, best and
Largest size.

Nicola Jerath (13)
Burscough Priory Science College, Burscough

Pups, Pups, Pups

More than forty pups
Have signed up,
Cold nose,
Warm heart,
Is the answer to your loneliness.

A spaniel called Spot,
Who enjoys choccie drops
Was matched with a cute little Dachshund
Who loves to play out.

There's Nicky from Swansea
Who's looking for his lady.
His personal favourite is to be pampered,
With a little help from me.

Ten pound per poochie,
Each with their Gucci,
Shampoos, clothes, sunglasses and more,
What more could the privileged pup want?

Sausage dog, Sparkle,
What more could you want?
You've got your own boy
Called Spotty, Spot, Spot.

Rex from Norwich,
Who sits in the sun,
Eating a great big iced bun,
Maybe you need a companion.

This doggy dating agency
Could be better than you think!

Jenny Evans (12)
Burscough Priory Science College, Burscough

The Two Towers

They stood so proudly side by side,
A symbol to the city,
Until an act of terrorism,
Came upon that city.

An aircraft hit the first tower,
Smoke billowed out,
The world stood by,
So terrified, unaware of what was to follow.

The disbelief that followed was
Greater than the last,
Horrified witnesses,
Watched as the second jet
Crashed into the second tower.

Horror, pain, panic,
That's all they felt that night,
Mourning for their loved ones,
Caused by an act of terrorism.

The world will never be the same,
The pain will never heal,
The things we saw that day,
Remains Ground Zero.

Holly Rothwell (12)
Burscough Priory Science College, Burscough

The Siege On Beslan

One Monday morning all happy and ready,
Older and younger children complete with teddy,
In brand new school uniforms, all glad to be back
And smiling teachers, new books all in stacks.

An apple for the teacher, a present for a friend,
Stories of summer which is now at an end,
Then came an army of men all of them masked,
All armed with machine guns ready to attack,
They escorted children and adults down to the gym,
All scared and confused, imprisoned within,
The men set traps all around the people,
Nowhere to go to eat or drink,
The hostages all just had to wait,
They waited three days, all used as bait,
Then came the Russian forces all anticipating and unnerved,
Some hostages ran out, these lives were spared.

Adults pulled children from debris, but it was too late,
For these little people it was their fate,
These terrorist beings are never to be forgiven,
As the future of Beslan is now in Heaven,
Whatever their wishes, their hopes or despairs,
These tragic deaths were never deserved.

Emma Craddock (12)
Burscough Priory Science College, Burscough

The Great North Run

Last Saturday was the Great North Run,
The run began with the sound of a gun.

Run runners, run,
Run, run, run.

Nearly 50,000 people ran through the town,
But only one person finished without a frown.

Run runners, run,
Run, run, run.

The only person happy was the winner of the race,
He passed the finish line with a smile on his face.

Run runners, un,
Run, run, run.

Dejene Berhanu was the winner's name
And he is very proud of all his fame.

Alex Rhodes (12)
Burscough Priory Science College, Burscough

My 9/11

I woke up excited for today I was getting a promotion,
I put on my work clothes and then put my coat on,
I set out for work, it was a beautiful morning,
Excited and ready for this day which was dawning.
I was walking along the sidewalk,
Feeling all enthusiastic,
Today was the perfect day, it was fantastic!
Suddenly there was a bang and I felt a whack,
Something had hit me, hard in the back,
Thousands of screams then filled the air,
Car horns, tumbling rocks, lots of people running around,
Flying debris falling to the ground,
Then another bang and both Twin Towers were falling down,
Swirling, curling black smoke was flying
And the cries of many people, the living and dying.

The events of that day will stick in my head,
My experience will stay with me until I am dead.

Bethan Caine (12)
Burscough Priory Science College, Burscough

Mini Men

There was once a man, a mini man,
He was round, small and fat!
He was green then blue, then red
And now he is as grey as a rat!
His name is Tomas Matter,
But his friends will call him Mat!
He was once in a dumper truck,
Trying to train a cat!
He now lives in a cave
And his best friend is a bat!
But now that he is dead,
He hasn't got a friend
And I can guarantee you this,
He will drive you round the bend!

Jack Jones (12)
Ellesmere Port Catholic High School, Ellesmere Port

My Wish

I wish I was a feline to roam and just be free
I would tease our neighbour's dog and then run up a tree
I could slip in people's windows and taste their Sunday lunch
I could watch the neighbours blame the dog and maybe get a punch

I could walk across the meadows, visit cows and pinch their cream
I could visit rabbits' burrows or paddle in the stream
I could lay on the rooftops and watch the traffic pass
I could watch my owner garden and then wee on the grass

I could get up when it suits me, or just stay in my bed
I would just rely on someone to make sure I am fed
I could stay out all day if I wanted to or maybe out all night
Though it's not a good idea, I'd just get in a fight

I could run across the main roads or on the railway track
Play havoc in the farmyard, chase rats around the stack
I would tease the bees and annoy them, pinch honey from their hives
Actually, I could do just what I wanted, I'm the cat that has nine lives!

Rebecca Hart (11)
Ellesmere Port Catholic High School, Ellesmere Port

Owls

The snowy owl has feathers so white
They live where it's cold, in places with snow
You only see them when they're out at night
With wings that are huge, they fly off and go
The barn owl, on the other hand, lives
In a barn with gloomy rafters and hay
The food it hunts, to the children it gives
They hunt all through the night and they sleep all through the day
The eagle owls have sharp, beady eyes
The live in the cliffs and build up their nest
Their ears are small compared to their size
Their hearing's not good, their sight is the best
All owls are said to be very wise
They're not! The only thing good is their eyes.

Jessica Hulse (12)
Ellesmere Port Catholic High School, Ellesmere Port

Hallowe'en

As I went walking in the forest green
I saw a sight that I had never seen
A group of witches standing round a fire
Their screaming voices were getting higher
I hid behind a tree and watched their moves
They summoned a devil with cloven hooves
As they were screaming, the forest it shook
I was frightened, I dared not look
The devil looked round with a piercing scream
Straight at the hiding place I had just been
For now I was running away from there
I had never had such an awful scare
No one would believe what I had just seen
I will never go back on Hallowe'en.

Alex Wasley (12)
Ellesmere Port Catholic High School, Ellesmere Port

Palm Trees

When the wind comes
The trees will sway
Sway will the palm trees
On a winter's day

When the wind didn't come
The trees stand still in the sun
Not a thing
Can disturb the statues

When the fierce wind comes
The statue's stillness is overrun
Swaying fiercely
In the wind

Swaying gently in the breeze
With the birds and the bees
She's sitting in the breeze
With the birds and the bees.

Ben Cameron (12)
Ellesmere Port Catholic High School, Ellesmere Port

Wind Wolf

He growls and whistles,
In despair,
On high mountains
Or in the air.

Soaring high
Or sweeping low,
He leaves no trace,
Where he may go.

Twisting, turning,
Towering high,
Up above,
In the shimmering sky.

Creeping, sneaking,
On the ground,
Moving swiftly,
With hardly a sound.

Bringing breezes,
From the clouds,
Crisp cold weather,
To chill the crowds.

The wind wolf,
Is everywhere,
In every breath,
Of the precious air.

Clare Nuttall (11)
Ellesmere Port Catholic High School, Ellesmere Port

Friendship

If you're tumbling down and your spirit falls
Don't worry, friendship is ready to stay
We're on our way, we'll answer your call
Reunited to make sure you're okay
All the lifelong time we'll be at your side
Put our heads together to find you
Our friendship is a roller coaster ride
Don't worry, everyone has had it too
You're not on your own, so have no doubt
We're all getting ready for your rescue
We'll find a way to get you straight out
Want to get out? Listen to your cue
Now you're out, let's get ready to party
Finished my poem, just call me Miss Poetry.

Emma Williams (12)
Ellesmere Port Catholic High School, Ellesmere Port

When I Got Told Off

When I got told off,
My teacher made a racket.
She kicked me through the door,
She put my head through a basket.

When my mum found out,
She smacked me really hard,
She sent me to the shed,
She made me sleep on card!

When my brother heard,
He laughed at me forever.
He bullied me all day,
He never stopped never, never, never!

I will never get told off,
Ever, ever, *ever!*

Georgina Jones (11)
Ellesmere Port Catholic High School, Ellesmere Port

The Mansion

We entered the mansion at midnight,
The place was such a gloom.
We stood in the hallway shivering,
When the door slammed, it was doom.

The lounge was covered in cobwebs,
The garden was splodged with mud.
The loft was swarming with spiders,
In the kitchen we saw blood!

I walked up the stairs with my sister,
Then she fell through the floor,
When I finally reached my bedroom,
I screamed when I opened the door.

There's a dead rat on the floorboard,
There's a skeleton in my bed.
I've had enough of this place,
Then a spider landed on my head.

We went down into the cellar,
When the clock struck half-past one,
A ghost appeared in its frightening way,
Now time to run.

Why are you running you chickens?
You are such a fool,
It was me, your sister, I did it,
I was the frightening ghoul.

Oh Sis, you are a meany,
We never had a clue.
But what is that so pale and white?
It's a ghost, it's a ghost, boo-hoo!'

Gregory Marsland (12)
Ellesmere Port Catholic High School, Ellesmere Port

The Ballad Of Tommy McCree

There's a tale from years ago
Of a boy called Tommy McCree
Stood in a park with his mates
A white bandage round his left knee

The moon was cold in the sky
It was a very dim, dark night
The green grass swayed in the wind
The stars in the sky shone bright

So this tale begins at last
The young boy crept out after bed
And ran down the tarmac road
Once in the field all was dead

Something in the bushes moved
The hairs on his neck stood on end
A pointy hat came in sight
A witch was there at Croswell bend

She grabbed the boy with a net
And tied his fingers to his toes
The wicked witch stared at him
Her eyes glared down her crooked nose

Suddenly she picked him up
And chucked him in the freezing lake
His body drowned in seconds
Someone help him for goodness sake!

Obviously the boy drowned
The very next day the news spread
At the bottom of that lake
Everyone left him for dead

I'm the ghost of Tommy McCree
I am here to set my spirits free.

Natalie Harding (13)
Ellesmere Port Catholic High School, Ellesmere Port

The House Next Door

I heard screaming last night, in the house next door,
It's where Mr Rogers lives with his brown dog.
I heard crashing and banging and shouts last night
And now he's disappeared like a frog.

The curtains have been drawn at the house next door,
The doors have been locked and the lights are switched off.
It's quiet as a mouse at the house next door,
No crashes or banging, not even a cough.

So then I decided to investigate,
I climbed through the dog flap and then searched the house.
But all I found was a bloodstained wooden spoon
And also the body of a dead grey mouse.

Then I realised that the screaming I heard,
Belonged to the man when he saw the grey mouse,
He battered and bashed it with the wooden spoon,
Now I know what went on at next door's brown house.

Laura Tolley (12)
Ellesmere Port Catholic High School, Ellesmere Port

Summer

Hooray, summer's back, coming once a year
The sun is shining and the sky is blue
The flowers are blooming and summer's here
The trees are swaying and full of leaves too
I like the paddling pools and water fights
And eating ice creams and lolly ices
Going on holidays, enjoying flights
And going to parties for cake slices
I can go ice skating any time now
But summer only comes one time a year
Spring is the season with the baby cows
But let's enjoy the summer while it's here
I like the winter, spring and autumn as well
But summer's my favourite, why, can't you tell?

Darcy Siegertsz (13)
Ellesmere Port Catholic High School, Ellesmere Port

Autumn Time

Autumn is here again, back to school
No!
Summer's ended now, rainy days are here
Conker season is here, so let us go
Dark nights are here, let's get the fear

Hallowe'en is near, get a suit to scare
Soon after this, it will be Bonfire Night
Fireworks will fly up in the air
Hallowe'en is here and there are some fights
Windy days are here so let their be fear
Rainy water is around, floody water is coming
It's so exciting, Christmas is near
Filled up with joy, Christmas carols humming

The summer might be over
And long gone
But for me, winter is the
Only one.

Thomas Fildes (12)
Ellesmere Port Catholic High School, Ellesmere Port

Thierry Henry

Thierry Henry, Thierry Henry
　　What a great goal
Great goal, great goal
　　That is Thierry Henry
Thierry Henry, Thierry Henry
　　How magic he is
He is, he is
　　Going to score a goal
A goal, a goal
　　What a wonder goal
Wonder goal, wonder goal
　　This is Thierry Henry.

Andrew Henry (12)
Ellesmere Port Catholic High School, Ellesmere Port

Jaguar

Jaguar, jaguar, how fast you are
A powerful, big and tall spotty blur
He bounds through the grass, amazingly far
The wind blowing its smooth silky fur.

Jaguar, jaguar, how proud you are
A confident and very strong animal
You even have the same name as a car
You are the greatest of all the mammals.

Jaguar, jaguar, how strong you are
As quiet as a whisper in the wind
Animals recoil from claws that can scar
Its power and strength it keeps tightly tinned.

A spotty wonder, an amazing thing
When it strikes, it's like a dagger that stings!

Adam Middleton (12)
Ellesmere Port Catholic High School, Ellesmere Port

Snow On A Winter's Day

Falling, freezing snow on a winter's day
Building Mr Snowman is so much fun
I'll get my hat, scarf and gloves to come play
Chucking snowballs while we're cold but we run
Blue toes and fingers, 'Mummy, help me please'
White-shaped things that are dropping from my nose
I'll sit by the fire, comfy on my knees
The camera's out, don't break it while I pose
The next morning when I wake up, it's gone
Watch the nature grow, it's back not so white
But it's still cold, so turn the heating on
It is getting hotter, I love the night
Snow is about, snowmen and so much cold
The snow will next come when I get so old.

Latiffa Cliffe (12)
Ellesmere Port Catholic High School, Ellesmere Port

The Little Rowboat

I sailed away to China,
On a little rowboat to find ya.

You said you had to get your laundry clean
And you smiled at me with gleam.

You wasted my time again,
Because you are a real pain.

My little rowboat floating on the seashore,
Which I drive with an oar.

You wanted to come home with me,
But I said you wouldn't be free.

I sailed back home to England,
So you went to sunny Finland.

I never saw you again
And your laundry was never clean.

Sophie McDonald (12)
Ellesmere Port Catholic High School, Ellesmere Port

My First Day At School

It was my first day at school
And I put on my cagool
I got in the car
While eating a chocolate bar
I saw tall teachers
And pretty pupils
We began our lunch
With a munch and a crunch
It was the end of play
As we made our way
Our first lesson was games
And I didn't know any names
It was the end of games.

Susannah Brumby (11)
Ellesmere Port Catholic High School, Ellesmere Port

Life

Life
It can be hard
It can be fun
But whatever happens
Your friends and family will help you through it

Make your choice
Right or wrong
Good or bad

But just remember
These things are all about growing up
Make the choice
No one can do it for you

It's your life!

Laura Abbate (11)
Ellesmere Port Catholic High School, Ellesmere Port

First Day At School

On my first day of school,
I looked like a complete fool,
At our first assembly,
I was very trembly,
Mr Lee was being a comedian,
Can you believe, my trousers were size medium?
I thought the teachers would be strict,
But Mr Thomas just took the mick,
At lunchtime the school looked so big,
But all we got was first day digs,
At the end of the day, I was in pain,
Just to think we have to go there again!

Conor Gilmour (11)
Ellesmere Port Catholic High School, Ellesmere Port

Nature

Nature is full of a wide range of plants
Trees are very big and they have leaves
Sug'ry plants are always covered in ants
Nature is fantastic, just ask Jeeves
I like watching upon a summer's day
Pink, purple, blue, colours of the rainbow
The smell of flowers makes me want to play
Pink petals of the flowers, watch them grow
Stop throwing glass bottles and crisp packets
Let the grass grow green and watch the birds fly
Don't be a muppet, throw them in a bucket
Watch the nature grow right in front of your eyes
Nature is about those fields and trees
And all of those creatures who squirm and scream.

Nathan Watson (12)
Ellesmere Port Catholic High School, Ellesmere Port

Chessboard

Our world is a great big chessboard,
We are all the same,
We should all work together as a family,
Racism is a big *no!*
We should not bully people,
Perfect people not aliens from another planet,
We should all be friends,
On a chessboard black and white are touching,
Whether black or white skin with a frown or a grin,
Well the Lord loves us all just the same.

Grace Taylor (11)
Ellesmere Port Catholic High School, Ellesmere Port

War Is Hell

The cold, dark, damp, rat-infested trenches
We will storm through no-man's-land and the barbed wire fences
I will soon fall slowly to the silent cold ground
And I will no longer make a sound
The blood is pouring out my freezing wound
England will soon be doomed
And as the soldier lay there to St Peter he will tell
'One more soldier reporting sir, I served my time in Hell.'

Daniel Smith (12)
Ellesmere Port Catholic High School, Ellesmere Port

Water

W ater, nice blue bubbly bath, warm or cold, the choice is yours!
A fter a long day you come up to a nice watery bath to
    warm your paws
T he rain is pouring, everyone gets wet, oh yes, don't forget . . .
    there's a bath upstairs and it's really nice
E ven though it's cold outside, nothing can spoil that lovely bath!
R rrr, that's so hot, I hope this bath never ends!

Robert Jones (12)
Ellesmere Port Catholic High School, Ellesmere Port

Hallowe'en

Goblins, monsters, witches that are green
Knock on your door each Hallowe'en
They walk the streets, in search of treats
Running around making scary sounds
Midnight comes and home they go
Where they come from
No one will ever know!

Shaun Mander (11)
Ellesmere Port Catholic High School, Ellesmere Port

Firework

Dancing and prancing they are going round,
Lighting up the sky and then they will go,
Smashing and dashing, making lots of sound,
Banging up the sky, they will go with one blow.

Fireworks have lots of types of colours,
People come to watch the firework displays.
They are all wrapped up in their warm jumpers,
Bonfire Night is great, we all count the days!

Sarah Warren (13)
Ellesmere Port Catholic High School, Ellesmere Port

The Fire

I have a fiery temper by the colour of my hair,
Everywhere is cold when I am not there.
I twist and I turn and fly towards the sky,
I can burn down houses and no one knows why,
I will spread and then I blow and destroy,
Then I go,
My hair as wire,
I am the fire!

Claire Craven (12)
Ellesmere Port Catholic High School, Ellesmere Port

I Hate Wasps!

I hate whizzing wasps
They hurt when they sting
They make me feel nervous
And they make me feel like hiding

It makes me feel like squashing them
Because they annoy me a lot
I wish I could sprout wings
But they are too fast to catch!

Krystal Watson (11)
Ellesmere Port Catholic High School, Ellesmere Port

Dolphins

Curious dolphins jump high and low
Hoping to catch funny, fast fish
As they catch the fast fish
They swallow all in one
Dolphins are beautiful creatures
And look so beautiful by their blue, smooth, silky body,
And their sharp, funny fin
I really enjoy watching them
And really want to join in.

Natalie Poole (11)
Ellesmere Port Catholic High School, Ellesmere Port

Shine Brightly

Shine like a star
Shining brightly all the time
Staying in the sky all night long
Moving around very slow

Always gleaming with the moon
Laughing in the night sky
The sun's coming up
Shining brightly all the time.

Rebecca Birchall (11)
Ellesmere Port Catholic High School, Ellesmere Port

My Butterfly Poem

Butterflies fly swiftly
Across the sky
Watch bright colours
Flash by.

Lucy McVeigh (12)
Ellesmere Port Catholic High School, Ellesmere Port

Hippo

A hippo, a hippo, I've got a pet hippo
He splashes in my baths
And he eats all my food
He's my pet hippo and he's kind of cool
A hippo, a hippo, I've got a pet hippo
I tuck him in at night when he gets a fright
He's my pet hippo and I've tucked him in tight
A hippo, a hippo, I've got a pet hippo
I took him swimmin', he scared all the women
He's my pet hippo and he's not the kind for slimmin'.

Charlotte Gray (13)
Ellesmere Port Catholic High School, Ellesmere Port

The Hedgehog

Rolling around the dusty old floor,
With its long, long nose,
Sniffling and snuffling,
Looking for something to eat before sunrise,
I really like hedgehogs,
But they carry lots of diseases,
Fleas and germs,
They prickle and sting
And make no noise at all,
You hardly know they are there.

Jade Griffiths (11)
Ellesmere Port Catholic High School, Ellesmere Port

The Tigerland

The Tigerland is where the armies clash
They do it for their country
They don't do it for the cash
They work all day and night
And hardly get any sleep
They drive around quite often
In a big 4x4 jeep

War day came quite quickly
Alert! Alert! Alert!
They fought all day
They fought all night
And many troops got hurt

The war was finally over
And all of the troops went home
Well, some of them anyway!

After all that fighting
In that terrible war
Some troops didn't make it alive
After all of the nightmares they'd been through
Some troops didn't survive

After the troops went home
Went to their families and cried
Because they knew inside their courageous heads
They were lucky to survive

60 years later
And only a few troops left
After all their nightmares
And horror in their life
In their memories the war will be kept!

Lewis Dodson (12)
Ellesmere Port Catholic High School, Ellesmere Port

My Poem About Two People Special To Me

I love my dad
As much as I love my mum
They are great parents to me
And always will

I live with my mum
At the weekends, I go to my dad's
I'm always happy when I'm with them
And always will

We live near each other
So that's one good thing
I'm happy where I live
And always will

Sometimes I'm sad
But not all of the time
I was sad when they got divorced
And always will

Sometimes they're mean
Making me do all the jobs
I hate doing them
And always will

They make me laugh
And have a brilliant time
They give me holidays
And always will.

Lyndsey Weeks (13)
Frodsham Science & Technology College, Frodsham

Scared To Talk

I hate the way you bully me,
You always call me names.
You laugh and laugh so I can see
And tease me with your games.
When I talk, you skit my walk,
You say I have no friends.
Because of you, I'm scared to talk,
It drives me round the bend.
When I go home and tell my mum,
She says, 'Just go on in!'
When I go through the gates they say, 'Come
And throw me in the bin.'
I'm scared to go to school and live,
I'm scared to talk . . .

Nicola Cunningham (13)
Frodsham Science & Technology College, Frodsham

Artemis Fowl

A rtemis Fowl who lives in a foreign land
R ummaging for fairies
T hat live underground
E lbows raised for combat
M agical rituals replenish their powers
I vory hunters you are on dangerous ground
S omething whizzed overhead

F airies, fairies everywhere
O vercome with fear
W ar was upon them, I'll
L eave the rest to your imagination.

Andy Perrin (12)
Frodsham Science & Technology College, Frodsham

Why Am I Different?

Whether I run or whether I walk,
Whether I sing or whether I talk,
There is one thing I'd like to say,
Why am I different? Explain one way!
Is it my hair? Is it my nose?
Is it my face? Is it my clothes?
Is it my voice or the way I speak?
Is it my strength? Is it because I'm weak?
I'm going to be brave, I'm really going to try,
To stand up to them, I'm not going to cry,
I stand here face to face with the worst of them all,
Is he going to punch me? Am I going to fall?
I'm going to be better, I'm sure that I will win,
I'm going to take his pride and throw it in the bin,
I've done it, I've won! I am the best,
That got the pressure right off my chest!

Jennie Hooper (13)
Frodsham Science & Technology College, Frodsham

Santa At Christmas

I like the way he eats the pies
And the way he slurps his drink
I like the way he moves his eyes
And doesn't look good in pink
I like the way he's always late
He makes me really bored
He moves his food around the plate
And plays cowboy with a sword
He always wears big black boots
And he always has a white beard
He's sometimes very weird
I also like the way he's old and fat
He always has a red hat.

Laura Lunny (13)
Frodsham Science & Technology College, Frodsham

Life Is A Life

(Inspired by 'Seven Ages of Man' by William Shakespeare)

Life is a mystery,
It's hard to solve.
Life is a villain,
Who takes the soul.
Life is a wonder
That's so very old!

Life has a meaning,
That we don't know.
Life is a treasure,
Don't throw it away.
Life is a life,
Be lucky to have one!

First comes the baby,
As sweet as candy.
His eyes bright
And soul, full of delight.
Now he has life!

Onto a toddler,
Ready to walk.
Falling over
And trying to talk
Because he has life!

He's at school now,
Learning to be a star.
If he tries hard,
He'll definitely go far.
He's glad he has life!

He's a teenager,
Getting grades and scoring As.
He wonders what he'll be
When he's grown up.
In his life!

As a man he succeeds,
At what he loves best.
Working on a relationship,
That'll surely be the best.
He's happy with his life!

An old man with hair grey,
He sits on a chair thinking.
It's been fun living my life,
Through twists and turns.
He's finally learnt that life is the best!

Life is a life!
Don't throw it away,
Live your life,
You'll see that it pays,
Not just in wage,
But in love, peace and happiness.
Therefore . . .
Life is a life!

Sammir Radha (13)
Frodsham Science & Technology College, Frodsham

The Way Of War

On toward the way, the way I travel,
Through the plain of death to my own demise,
Marching across the path of the gravel,
Knowing that we're watched from sinister eyes,
The sounds of guns are in the distance,
The bodies of the dead beneath my feet,
All the men falling within an instance,
Trailing through the sand beneath the desert heat,
All the regiments moving for the fight,
All the enemies moving for the battle,
All the forces are ready for the flight,
We're all being rounded up like cattle,
All of this war, it all just seems senseless,
I want to live my life free and fenceless.

Ben Davies (13)
Frodsham Science & Technology College, Frodsham

Going Over The Top

Fears are high,
Trenches far from dry,
Dug in ditch,
I'm far from rich!

Going over the top

Uniform clean,
Gun looking mean,
Sleeping cold,
Eating mould!

Going over the top

The rat that looms,
The firing booms,
It will never stop,
Like a constant pop!

Going over the top

The battle of the Somme,
Is far from calm,
We won't die in vain,
Long live our country's reign!

Going over the top.

Stephen Smith (14)
Frodsham Science & Technology College, Frodsham

Snow Haiku

Snowdrops falling down
Landing lightly on my head
Say that winter's come.

Katy Ingram (13)
Frodsham Science & Technology College, Frodsham

Should It Be This Way?

Why did they lie?
Why did they cheat?
What did they gain?
Who did they beat?

Answers are what we want
And our troops home,
But how do we do that
Without leaving Iraq alone?

Why did he get the vote
When he caused all this mess?
Why did they choose him?
Why did they say yes?

He needs to accept it,
He needs to see sense.
Yes we have him,
But at whose expense?

I know he hurt them,
I know he should pay,
But the victims shouldn't suffer,
It shouldn't be this way.

Emily Hignell (14)
Frodsham Science & Technology College, Frodsham

My Poem

He's mad as a hatter
He's got all the patter
A criminal mastermind
Planning to rob you blind
Tread careful Holly Short
Or you will get caught
Secrets will be lost
Their fairy wings will turn to frost
Because the four winds howl
The name of Artemis Fowl.

Jack Wilson (11)
Frodsham Science & Technology College, Frodsham

Christmas

Opening the presents, tearing off the wrapping,
Excited children, laughing and clapping.
That's just what I wanted, hooray, hooray,
Christmas Day is the very best day!

Then when all the presents have been opened up,
It's Mum's job to tidy up.
She watches the children play with their toys,
Just like good little girls and boys.

Christmas is over, the magic has gone,
The spark has disappeared of a candle that once shone.
Children's laughter has faded away,
But Christmas will come another day.

Melissa McGowan (14)
Frodsham Science & Technology College, Frodsham

I Wish

I wish upon a Christmas star,
That he will come despite how far.

I wish upon a Christmas spell,
That I will hear his reindeer's bell.

I wish upon a Christmas tree,
That he will bring a gift for me.

I wish upon a Christmas card,
That snow will fall, fall really hard.

But what my Christmas wish should really be,
Is for peace on Earth, for all men and me.

Laura Berry (13)
Frodsham Science & Technology College, Frodsham

Gang War

The fire was burning in the misty fog
They approached cautiously with guns and knives
The enemy came up and began to jog
They both threatened to kill each other's wives
The pair of gangs attacked with no remorse
Towards the gang leader to slice and dice
The back line invaded with lots of force
We threatened to kill like cats chasing mice
I walked in silence with a baseball bat
It was a perfect place, no one in sight
Our leader was killed and that was that
Their flag stood tall in the wind like a kite
I don't believe it, I have taken her life
What's the point living without my wife?

Jake Hardman (14)
Frodsham Science & Technology College, Frodsham

Feelings

I have many feelings,
They have different meanings,
Some are crazy,
Some are sad,
Some are happy,
Some are bad,
Some I understand,
Some I don't,
Each of these feelings
Which have meanings
Some of these feelings I show
May upset those I know.

Rachelle Carter-Shepherd (14)
Frodsham Science & Technology College, Frodsham

Billy

My life is hard
My home is bare
I go to work
But no one's there
I have no friends
Nowhere to go
I want a friend
They all say no
I buy my food
I eat alone
I call for someone
I use the telephone
But still I keep looking
Trying night and day
Cry myself to sleep
Even nerds say no way
So here I am
Still on the search
Just like the past year
Day by day and night by night
All it takes is just one friend.

Daniel Pacheco (14)
Frodsham Science & Technology College, Frodsham

The Prisoner

I walk to the window in my cell,
I heard the call from the king,
The executioner rang the bell,
The axe was sharp,
The stone was brought,
The drums were beating,
A glint of the sword and
Huh, he's dead, the head rolled around,
The executioner after the head.

Joshua Solari (13)
Frodsham Science & Technology College, Frodsham

It's A Girl's World

High street shops and the most fashionable labels
Skimpy skirts and the eyes of flirts
Welcome to a girl's world
Slap on the make-up
And spritz on the spray
Welcome to a girl's day

Flutter those eyelashes
Wiggle that bum
It's all part of having fun
Welcome to a girl's world
Pout those lips
And blow a kiss
Receive a whistle
And a cheesy wink
Welcome to a girl's day

There they go again
Passing notes
It's about me
I can tell by the dirty looks
Welcome to a girl's world
Be a cow
And have a bitch
But pretend like you're not a witch
Welcome to a girl's day!

Welcome to a girl's world
You'll wanna live our life
That's all I can say!

Ameira-Louise Hasoun (13)
Frodsham Science & Technology College, Frodsham

Herod

(Inspired by Carol Ann Duffy's 'Salome')

Well done Salome
You're dancing good
You looked pretty
Just like you should

I was watching
A lad wanted a kiss
You deserve my offer
Of giving you a wish

I'll have to go
To discuss it with my mum
The one over the road
With the big bum

I want a bit of John
John the Baptist's head
When you have got it
Bring it to my shed

How will I get
How will I cut it off?
Maybe I'll slip
When I cough

That's a good idea
I'll do it ASAP
Then I'll have the head
For Salome to see

There you go
It was as easy as pie
I wonder if she knows
I'm telling a lie.

Dean Ratcliffe (13)
Frodsham Science & Technology College, Frodsham

Technological Nirvana

'A technological Nirvana - Earth
Reborn to humans, power of ours,
Controls this place that we lived since birth,
Now the robots' turn to gaze on God's arms.

The artificial creatures hypnotise,
The humans in carrying out the chores,
Transforming this land to a paradise,
Then soon shall man be cast from Heaven's doors.

Raging storms tear through this mystical sky,
Like a psychopath caged behind steel bars,
Now for the humans to say goodbye,
Then will we creatures be banished to Mars?

Earth is just torture, suffering and pain,
Just a scheming robot's twisted game.

Daniel Collinson (13)
Frodsham Science & Technology College, Frodsham

Final Battle

This is my final battle
I will make my country proud
Even though I will pass away
And surrender beyond the clouds
It is my duty to serve my country
With dignity and with pride
My heart is breaking slowly
As I go on my final ride
I love you all more than you know
So goodbye my friends
Goodbye my country, goodbye my family
I will see you in the later life
If you wish me to.

Alex MacGugan (14)
Frodsham Science & Technology College, Frodsham

Herod

(Inspired by Carol Ann Duffy's 'Salome')

Why can't I sleep?
Is it John?
Was I right to give Salome her wish?
Was it her wish?
It was a spectacular dance
But it was only a dance
I could not give away my respect
Not in front of guests
I wish John was still here
I didn't want him alive
But I certainly didn't want him dead

No one will oppose me now
Not over Herodias
I wouldn't have minded killing someone
To prove my love
But John didn't deserve to die.

Gareth Miller (14)
Frodsham Science & Technology College, Frodsham

My Best Friend

My best friend
Cooks and cleans
And always makes me feel at ease

My best friend
Like a bear
Is warm and cuddly and cares

My best friend
As if she's the sun
Keeps me bright as sunlight

My best friend
Is my mum.

Katie Stubbs (13)
Frodsham Science & Technology College, Frodsham

Killer

I walked in silence with a baseball bat
    It was perfect, she was asleep in bed
It all went wrong, I was seen by her cat
    I struck her not once but twice 'cross the head
The blood seeped out of her open head wound
    There was a knock upon her rusted door
Her lips turned blue as her stomach ballooned
    I jumped cos of the sound and struck her once more
I needed to escape from this weary house
    Nowhere to run, nowhere to hide, I was scared
I could not be loud, I'd got to creep like a mouse
    The room's door opened and at the man I stared
This murder is one which is nothing but bad
    The person that killed her must have been mad.

Jake Garner (14)
Frodsham Science & Technology College, Frodsham

Spoil Me!

I like to hear your money *ching*
When you're buying me loads of bling

I want diamonds and rubies
Silver and gold

I like being spoilt
It never gets old

Trackies and trainees may be nice!
But I want labels and all your ice.

Don't spend all your riches on all your bitches,
See this through and I'll be your beau!

Alex Flood (14)
Frodsham Science & Technology College, Frodsham

Young Love

What a liar,
Such a cheat,
What he said,
Such a fake,
Did he mean it?
So he says,
I can't see it,
Was it just a phase,
I want to just wake up
And for it all to be a dream,
I lie in bed at night
And I just want to scream,
Why did he do this to me?
Why did he make me cry?
Why did he say those three little words?
Why did he lie?
Now I am here with a broken heart,
Was it my fault that it all fell apart?
He seems to have moved on already,
I mustn't have meant that much
Are we still going to be friends?
Will we stay in touch?
Who's to know what the future holds,
He said we'd be together as we grew old,
Now that's all gone down the drain,
Why did he cause me so much pain?

Ashleigh Fry (13)
Frodsham Science & Technology College, Frodsham

Goodbye To The World

Lying here,
Drowned in red,
No hopes or dreams,
I am near dead.

My time has come
And I wonder why,
What was so bad,
That I wanted to die?

Now there is
No turning back,
Light-headed, dizzy,
Because of blood I lack.

The blade still in my hand,
As the night grows old,
Getting more dark
And getting more cold.

As I breathe,
My final breath,
It's obvious that
I caused my death.

I blink once more,
Then shut my eyes,
Goodbye to the world
And to my life.

Rachel Foreman (13)
Frodsham Science & Technology College, Frodsham

Life According To Me

My years may be few, but in your eyes,
Each word that I speak is nothing but lies.
Because of my age, you think less of me,
But do not judge me by others you see.

My years may be few, but that does not mean,
That the views that I hold don't deserve to be seen,
I may be young, but my age doesn't state
That someone but me may control my fate.

During my 15 short years I have learned,
That respect is not given, respect is earned.
Things I have been taught will remain with me here,
But lessons will fade with each passing year.

Please look beyond these youthful tears
And help those who need it to defeat their fears.
If you have feelings that you don't try and hide,
Stop, take a look and see what's inside.

Do not judge me by others you see,
Others you see do not reflect me,
Each of us love, think and feel,
But judge us for us. That is what's real.

So as the seconds and hours pass by,
Don't think of my words as lie after lie,
Watch the day fade with tick after tock,
Look at the person, not at the clock.

Jenna Johnston (15)
Frodsham Science & Technology College, Frodsham

Revised Dreams

Galloping up to the very last fence,
Urging Meg on, quicker, quicker,
The jump drawing closer, closer and closer.

Something quick, darting in front,
Meg rearing, bucking, out of control,
Rearing again,
This time too far,
Falling, falling,
To the ground we fall.

A dead weight lifted,
As she got up,
I can't move,
I'm lying in pain.

People running, shouting, screaming,
Light flashing all around me,
My dreams lost,
My hopes flattened,
But not gone forever.

Zara Gerrard (13)
Frodsham Science & Technology College, Frodsham

Do Not Bully

D on't you dare,
O ne push and

N o friends you'll have,
O ne day you'll see
T hat bullying

B ugs me,
U don't understand,
L ook around,
L ove is on the way,
Y ou deserve it.

Joshua Kennils (11)
Frodsham Science & Technology College, Frodsham

I Don't Belong

School is such a dreadful place,
So many people,
So much to face.

I felt intimidated,
Lost in a crowd,
People were so nasty,
I wanted to shout out loud.

A silent scream from one to another,
No one understood,
Not even my mother.

They're waiting for me over there,
I can feel the burn of their intense stare.

Would he punch me or let me fall?
Pinned to the ground or pressed against the wall.

But they pushed and pulled me and dragged me along,
I know what they thought,
I didn't belong.

Well it doesn't matter anymore,
I'm now approaching the large wooden door,
I'm nearly there,
Only seconds to go,
Don't tell anyone, only you and I know.

I'm there now,
The place in the sky,
I look back and I don't know why.

I could have stood up to them,
I could have made it stop,
They were too persistent,
This is what they've got.

Hannah Pierce (13)
Frodsham Science & Technology College, Frodsham

Stuff The Turkey!

It was the night before Christmas and all through the house,
Not a creature was stirring not even a mouse
And as the children retired to bed,
The parents worried about the day ahead.

The only thing that didn't seem right
Was the big bright star shining so bright
And as the parents retired to bed,
They could do nothing but think of the debt ahead.

So the doorbell rings and the family arrives;
This joyous day brings a lot of surprise.
You look at your children. That glint in their eye,
But was it all worth it? I hear you all cry.

The big turkey dinner and the presents you have had,
Cannot replace the feeling of guilt you have,
The paper in shreds, the cards on the floor,
What was the point in this? Who was it for?

The curtains will close, the sky will be grey,
This Christmas will be over hip hip hooray
And the children will realise when their time arrives,
Just what it is like to plan such an expensive surprise.

You will walk down the street among all of the shops
And kick yourself in the shin when you see all the drops,
The prices will be lowered, the stress will be gone,
But the children will argue, 'I want that one.'

So why do we do it, year after year?
It gets more expensive, we buy much less beer,
The kids still aren't grateful, the presents are all broken,
The festivities all gone but the bank manager's choking.

The debt has increased, the stress has returned,
You'll work all this year to give what you've earned.

Steph Oscroft (17)
Frodsham Science & Technology College, Frodsham

Herod

(Inspired by Carol Ann Duffy's 'Salome')

Oh no, this isn't good
I didn't mean to kill the man
But she was such a good dancer . . .
An oath though
Isn't that a bit far?
But then there's Herodias
She wanted him to die
I didn't think Salome would ask for that
But as loyal as ever
To ask for a head on a platter

I swore I'd give her
What she wanted
What did I care?
But what about
The executioner?
Responsible for killing
Such a holy man . . .
The cousin of the Messiah
But to ask for a head on a platter?

Robert Ward-Dutton (13)
Frodsham Science & Technology College, Frodsham

Darkness In The Hearts

The darkness in the hearts,
So many don't see the pain,
Because it's not on home soil,
They never see the rain.

After the slaughter has ended
And so many have died,
Will the pain and suffering,
Ever stop or subside?

So many are in mourning,
So many families cry,
Life on the battlefield,
They can and do die.

Scottish families,
The Blackwatch soldiers dream
Of those better days,
Then it's broken by a scream.

Children in those countries,
They'll never see peace,
Soldiers fighting all the time,
Give them a childhood at least.

Johanna Pickering (14)
Frodsham Science & Technology College, Frodsham

Ratalogue

Rats sleep curled up and walk slow,
When they wake, they stretch and yawn,
Their whiskers twitch
And they sleep in a ball.

Rats eat quite fast,
They lick themselves clean,
Rats have small pink paws like miniature human hands.

Rats have . . .
Creamy white fur,
Pink, little wet noses,
Dark red eyes which stare,
Cute faces
And silky ears.

Rats drink lots and lots,
Their tongues work hard to slurp the water,
They have long tails which drag along,
Rats are cute and friendly, don't get them wrong!

Amy Hammond (11)
Mostyn House School, South Wirral

Sherbet Lemons

Bright yellow oval sweet
Wrapped up in a yellow treat
Fizzy sherbet pouring into my mouth
Tickling my tongue on the way
Size of a thumb the lemon sherbet moving
Around in my mouth
Sour as a lemon and lime
Crunching, munching as I crunch the sweet
You get a lemon taste after.

Lauren Morgan (11)
Mostyn House School, South Wirral

Autumn

Autumn is fireworks,
Lighting up the midnight sky.
Autumn to me is leaves,
Falling off the trees.
When I think of autumn,
I think of Hallowe'en.

What is autumn?
Autumn is sticks,
Burning on the bonfire.
Autumn is birds pecking
At the berries on the trees.
Autumn to me is mischievous night,
Getting up to no good.

When I think of autumn I think of
Drinking hot chocolate in the dark.
Autumn is bright colours,
Colours showing on the trees.
Autumn to me is playing,
Games with conkers.

Rebecca Hanmer & Rachel McDonald (11)
New Heys Comprehensive School, Liverpool

Music

Music is a way of life
It describes your inner self
Without music who would you be?
It clears your path and helps you see
It helps you through the times you hate
Although some people think it's too late
The lyrics are like a way out
They take away the pain which cries out
To some people music is everything.

Vicky Williams (14)
New Heys Comprehensive School, Liverpool

The Star

The
star that
shines up, up high
is like a diamond glowing bright.
It twinkles golden yellow, like a rainbow in the sky.
A tiny sun giving warm beams, that I wish to touch, so
small yet big. I reach out to
touch that sparkly, pointy star. But
I can't reach,   it's not fair.
That pointy star   that longs to
be touched, once   more let down
by a child   no older
than   eight.

Alice Williams (11)
New Heys Comprehensive School, Liverpool

Summer Night's Dream

I lie dreaming in Iraq
Looking at the golden sun.

I dream of the sound of the river flowing,
As the green grass is growing.

I dream of the birds waking me up,
As the scent of the flowers takes me to Heaven.

I dream of the sound of my happy children,
Where, no matter where I am, I am always in their hearts.

I wake to the sound of gunshot -
And realise it is only a dream.

Amy Green (12)
New Heys Comprehensive School, Liverpool

Gothic Discrimination

People think that I'm a freak,
Because I dress in black,
But this is how I choose to live,
Respect my decision, accept me for what I am.

I look into the mirror
And all I see is me,
I couldn't be any happier,
This is how I want to be.

Funny looks on the way to school,
Because I don't dress in a way that's socially mainstream,
It's like a form of racial abuse,
They think I'm some sort of Satanist,
But there's more to it than there seems.

Trapped in a place that I couldn't get out of,
Hiding from demons that didn't exist.
Falling through darkness with no destination,
A constant victim of Gothic discrimination.

Paul Roberts (14)
New Heys Comprehensive School, Liverpool

Africa

Africa is a peaceful place to be,
Waterfalls, safari and me,
Hunger strike, no water, poorly things,
Not even any money to buy a ring,
Craft and art, loud music,
Everyone asks how to use it,
Lovely views, funny kids,
Not even a half of biscuit to spare,
Nobody even cares,
Wild animals, no food or drink,
But sooner or later for them,
What do you think?

Rebecca Blackall (11)
New Heys Comprehensive School, Liverpool

Liverpool Compared To Bolton

Bolton Wanderers are world . . . crap,
Liverpool are world . . . class.
We were treble winners 2000-2001,
All Bolton are in a big con,
We won the Champions League 1984 and many more,
Bolton find it hard to score.
We have the Spanish superstars,
What planet does Jaidi come from? Mars.
We have super Stevie Garrod,
Bolton have Ricardo Gardner,
We are the red army,
Bolton are all crap and barmy.
We have Anfield,
Bolton can't even get to the Charity Shield.
The red and white all around,
Bolton get a bonus of a pound.
We have Xabi (the amazing) Alonso,
Bolton will end up signing Tore Andre Flo.
Super Jay-Jay who?
We have Harry Kew.
Bolton love big Sam,
Liverpool are always on Player Cam.
We are defo a Champions League team,
Bolton are wools and play in cream,
We have had great managers like Bill Shankley, Bob Paisley,
Bolton run around collecting daisies,
We have had a French flop,
But at least we have had the Kop.

Craig Dineley (14)
New Heys Comprehensive School, Liverpool

Rain Haiku

Clouds getting heavy
Puddles cover all the land
Like carpets of silk.

Laura Tickle (12)
New Heys Comprehensive School, Liverpool

The Bell Tower

Up in the bell tower way up high,
There lurks a shadow that can't be seen by the naked eye,
By day he lurks up in the bells,
At night he comes to cast his spells,
For when the moon appears through the windows,
To the outside world he goes,
To catch his prey for the night,
He uses his incredible sight,
He leaps into a farmer's yard,
For a quick snack, it isn't hard,
Out he stalks with a blood-soaked muzzle,
Where the sheep have gone is the farmer's puzzle,
Morning is nigh
And he howls, 'Why?'
As the transformation begins
And he thinks of his sins,
He runs back to his tower,
For now he's lost all his power,
He hangs his head in sorrow,
But he knows it will all happen again tomorrow.

Cara McPartland (11)
New Heys Comprehensive School, Liverpool

The View

I am sitting there watching the world go by,
I can see all sorts, birds, people, babies that cry,
My life changes when I see everything,
That not everyone gets to see.
Part of me feels happy and part of me feels sad.
I don't understand,
Nature flies everywhere,
Kids play in the park,
Adults talking about their relationships,
Everyone is happy,
I can see it at the view of the world.

Hannah Langley (11)
New Heys Comprehensive School, Liverpool

Shadows

It's there again, stuck to the soles of my feet
Why does it follow me?
Creeping up enlarging any object to make it look terrifying
It was summoned by the sun, all the sun's little dark soldiers
It's still following me, it won't leave me alone
It's my own personal stalker and I can't file a complaint
Sometimes when the sun goes down, it sinks down into the ground
But I soon find that the sun and the moon are a tag team
And up rise the dark soldiers for another time
It's sneaking up on me, I can't stop it
I hide in the dark corner and it disappears
Where could it be? When it seems clear I step out from
The dark corner and out jumps the dark figure
I need to escape, I want to close my eyes
But I need to keep my eye on it to stop it from getting me
I bet you never thought a shadow could be so scary!

Kelly Walker (11)
New Heys Comprehensive School, Liverpool

Through The Valley Haiku

Leaves falling off trees,
On beautiful cottages
And the cobbled road.

Lucy Roberts (12)
New Heys Comprehensive School, Liverpool

Autumn Leaves Haiku

They fall steadily
Stunning colours, gold, red, brown
They lie there lonely.

Harriet Dunne (12)
New Heys Comprehensive School, Liverpool

Sail Away Grandad

The time was ticking, then the clock stopped
You fought for so long
But now it was time to give up
For months I saw you fade to a shadow of the man you were
But you were always my grandad
And always will be, no matter what the turn
Seven kids you brought to this world
Twenty grandkids you were given back
I look now in the house where the family was raised
Even when I can't see you, I think back to the happy days
The days where you'd tell me sailing war stories
And fill my body with laughter
I miss them now more than ever
Some days I feel I need you more than ever
The family you made were heartbroken
On the day you said goodbye
But you sailed away to a better place
When I need you I simply smile and look up to the sky!

Joanne McCann (14)
New Heys Comprehensive School, Liverpool

Liverpool Haiku

Liverpool is great
A city alive with fun
A place we call home.

Jade Wright (12)
New Heys Comprehensive School, Liverpool

Tiger Haiku

The lonely tiger
Stared at me with his big eyes
He hated the zoo.

Danekka Widdows (12)
New Heys Comprehensive School, Liverpool

All About My Friend

She was very kind
And very nice,
She used to smoke,
But then she knew it wasn't good for you,
She wears glasses.

She's a habit of reading things,
Like jigsaws, magazines,
She can't go out and watch leaves cartwheel,
She has a very ill husband,
Takes care of him really well.

She was very useful at helping people,
But now she's got a bad back,
Walking stick helps her to walk,
Still a nice person,
I wish I knew her longer.

Jake Lovatt (13)
St Wilfrid's Catholic High School, Liverpool

Grandad's Pipe

The smell was strong
And the smoke was dark,
My grandad lit up his pipe
On the cold winter nights,
Banging the ash on the side
Of the warm fire,
The stem was chewed,
As he took the
First long slow pull.

Hayley Maguire (13)
St Wilfrid's Catholic High School, Liverpool

What Justice Means To People

Everyone is equal,
No matter black or white,
No matter the distance between them,
They'll always put up a fight,
Justice?
Is life fair?
Jealousy, religion, colour of skin,
Everyone is part of one society,
Closer together than they thought,
Some people have dreams,
Some people live life as it comes,
The rich and the poor,
They're all equal,
So I ask you,
Is life fair?

Sarah McClements (14)
St Wilfrid's Catholic High School, Liverpool

Hell Box

(Based on 'Magic Box' by Kit Wright)

In my Hell box I would find . . .
A flying beast that I will fly away on
A giant robot that will obey me
A time watch that will take me to the past
An army that will protect me at any cost
An everlasting money bag that lasts 100 years
A miniature tornado that gobbles people up
A fast car that can go faster than light.

Conor Critchley (12)
St Wilfrid's Catholic High School, Liverpool

Grandad

Whilst sitting in his old brown rocking chair,
Rocking away,
He'd smoke his pipe on dark evenings,
The smoke would curl and swirl,
It was thick although not heavy,
But still floated along with the thin air,
His habits charmed me,
One after another,
Slightly banging the ash within the coal,
It would never harm me switching channels,
A constant search throughout the channels,
Searching through the football results,
A dreadful gloom at the television,
Daydreaming,
His glasses would slide to the tip of his nose,
Tired eyes staring at the television,
Slowly, dreadfully, eyes shut.

Stephanie Phenna (13)
St Wilfrid's Catholic High School, Liverpool

My Pop

5 o'clock strikes,
Pop walks through the door,
The smell of food flows through the house,
As Pop wipes his feet on the floor.
Into the living room by his favourite chair
Would be two bacon butties
And a strong cup of tea.
After his food he'd reach for his pipe,
Take a few pulls and let out a sight.
He'd fall asleep silently in his chair by the fire,
This is his favourite Thursday routine,
Though he's gone right now,
His habits still charm me.

Sophie Hoy
St Wilfrid's Catholic High School, Liverpool

My Grandad

My grandad while sitting there
In his chair he would
Take a pull of his pipe
With a chewed bitty end

The thick smell filled the
Whole room with heavy smoke
Smoke curled up
Words into the light

His pipe was long and thin
Brown and it was smelly
As he tapped his pipe
The ash fell and crumbled
Into the fireplace

Then he sat and lay back
And took a long slow pull
Of his pipe.

Michael Fitzsimmons (13)
St Wilfrid's Catholic High School, Liverpool

I Miss

I miss his house
I miss his street
I miss the food
I miss the dog
I miss the garden
I miss the fish
I miss the way he did things
But the one thing
I miss the most is my grandad.

Paula Dryhurst (13)
St Wilfrid's Catholic High School, Liverpool

My Grandad's Past

My grandad sat in his brown wooden chair,
Smoking from his pipe and reading his paper.
He would sit there for hours chewing his stem
And reading about horse racing.
His glasses would slide down his face
And his pipe would burn in his hand.
The house smelt of strong tobacco,
For he blew the smoke out of his mouth.
It would linger around the room
Until it faded into thin air,
Fading into our clothes and the past.
His dog, a golden Labrador,
Would sit by the fire on guard,
Protecting my grandad.
My grandad would have a picture
On his mantelpiece of his family,
He would gaze on at the picture
As he told us stories of the past.
He would sit there reaching for his wallet,
In his pocket, where he would count how much
He had and how much pension he would have.
Rustling his notes and clanging his coppers
Like a big bass drum.
Staring on at the telly
Catching his football results,
Grandad's glasses would slide down his face,
Landing on the bottom of his nose.
He would have a cackling cough,
Pushing them back on the bridge of his nose.
My nan would carefully walk in from the kitchen
With two warm cups of tea,
They would both pick up the cup
And sip, then gulp, placing the cups down
They would talk to one another about their day.
My grandad is the oldest person I know
And I would never change him,
For he is loving, caring, kind and my best friend.

Louise Brash (13)
St Wilfrid's Catholic High School, Liverpool

Nanny Sadie

The chimeless grandfather clock hangs on her wall,
Waiting to be wound up,
The annoying tick-tock of the clock disturbs the silent living room,
Though it wasn't clear to me,
That clock was over 50 years old.

The useless LP player sits with the rusty old LPs
In the corner of the back room,
I remember Nanny Sadie using it, but only once.

7 children she has and 11 grandchildren
And 2 great grandchildren,
4 boys and 3 girls,
Robert, Dave, Peter and Paul were the boys,
Gillian, Paula and Debbie were the girls.

Her husband, Robert, who died of cancer, I never met,
Nanny Sadie is funny, that probably came from Grandad,
He was only 49 when he died,
Such a young age to die,
He died 2 days after my brother was born.

My nan used to work in the Heritage Market,
When it was a tobacco factory,
She worked there for twenty years,
That's probably why she smoked a lot.

Even though my nan is old
And has had diabetes for nineteen years,
She's still a laugh,
She moans a lot,
But who doesn't?

David Martlow (13)
St Wilfrid's Catholic High School, Liverpool

My Grandad

The sun beams down
And melts his ice cream
The temperature is hot
In Lanzarote

The swoosh of the sea
The sand between my toes
A gentle breeze
As he sits by the sea

He'll have drink after drink

The cold beer floating down his throat
The sweat dripping off his forehead
All alone
As he takes a dip in the pool

There he goes on the plane
Checking the football results
With the cigar at the end of his mouth
The smoke flows through the thin air.

Emma Golding (13)
St Wilfrid's Catholic High School, Liverpool

A Special Person

Her house, a stale smell of cigarettes clouded around the rooms,
In the front room a chair that she uses as her bed,
Cigarettes are no longer there,
Now her new hobby is eating and sucking on her mints all day,
The smell of smoke lurking in the room's air.

She doesn't go out much,
She only goes to the shop.

Lee Morris (13)
St Wilfrid's Catholic High School, Liverpool

My Nan Yvonne

My nan is 55 years old,
Her husband is 57 years old,
She had a dog called Sam,
She has a rabbit called Thumper.

She reads a prayer every night,
Some are from newspapers,
Some are from books,
Some are old,
Some are new.

She works in a shop called Classic Menswear,
For eveningwear and wedding hire.

She wears glasses but can never find them,
Losing them in the most unusual places.

She likes to cook and clean,
She's also great fun, playing games all the time,
She's always very caring,
But can sometimes be embarrassing.

But the best thing is that she is very fit,
Always making sure she does her exercises.

Kyle Law (13)
St Wilfrid's Catholic High School, Liverpool

Grandad's Pipe

The stem of the old wooden pipe was chewed,
There were teeth marks at the bottom of the pipe,
He banged the thick ash on the fireplace,
The smoke from the pipe was huge
And it curled through the air getting bigger and bigger,
Before the smoke slowly disappeared into the air.

Matthew O'Connell (14)
St Wilfrid's Catholic High School, Liverpool

My Nanny Joan

My nan went to the shop every day,
She'd come home with a box of cigarettes in her hand,
A box of 10 Berkeley Red,
My nan loved her cigarettes,
She would go into the kitchen
And stand there in the doorway and have one.

My nan's parlour is a deserted room,
It would only come alive when her granddaughters
And grandsons came to her house and played in there,
When lonely or bored, she would go into the room
And watch TV.

My nan has pictures everywhere, downstairs and upstairs,
I look at them as I walk around her house,
When I see lots of pictures of families,
They remind me of my Nanny Joan.

Warren Lavery (13)
St Wilfrid's Catholic High School, Liverpool

Grandad John

When Grandad comes to visit
He always has a glass,
'Just to warm up my bones,'
He strongly bellows out,
I watch him take a small dose,
Then a loud clang as his hands clasp together,
They are swiftly rubbed.
I buy him a bottle every Christmas,
Grandad truly adores his bottle of Bells.
A £10 note always lies upon the mantelpiece,
Waiting for an excited face to stare straight at it,
There's always one left for me,
Every time that face is mine.

Laura Pugh (13)
St Wilfrid's Catholic High School, Liverpool

Auntie Mal

My auntie is called Marrion,
Sometimes we call her Mal,
Sometimes at tea we have cake
She bought the day before.

We go to her flat every Saturday
And play with little Phil,
We play football and he gets excited,
He always wets his pants.

When she was in a good mood,
She would hide her keys,
We would play a game to get them back,
She'd give us a lot of sweets.

She's a little soft in the head,
She thinks she has a dog called Ted,
Mal always tucks him into bed,
But little does she know, his name is really Fred.

Lauren Lovatt (13)
St Wilfrid's Catholic High School, Liverpool

Evil Passing By

There is evil in the world
It is everywhere
Every time I walk I see evil staring at me
I don't dare to stare back
Every time I go out I feel it passing by
Even when I turn the TV on
There is evil, hatred and death
You hear that people have died
You just feel that you want to cry.

Chris Marsland (14)
St Wilfrid's Catholic High School, Liverpool

Howard Walsh

Howard Walsh loved football especially Everton,
He smoked his cigars and cigarettes every day,
Still got round a lot even though he had a bad limp
And had a walking stick,
Always went to the bookies but if not,
He got his son to go and put a bet on for him,
He loved to watch the horseracing,
Loved to watch the lottery even though
He knew he wasn't going to win,
He liked making jokes on his intercom,
He would pretend to break up on it
And people would fall for it
But they took it in and laughed.

Terence Hartley (13)
St Wilfrid's Catholic High School, Liverpool

My Uncle Eddie

My uncle always held the remote on his reclining chair
Looking through the TV guide to see what's on for kids
If there was a match on, we wouldn't watch it
We could watch what we wanted
While he put his chair in the back position
And had a midday nap
His favourite day was Sunday
He would let us lie in and then we had a fried breakfast
He went for his Sunday walk
And came back with a paper and lots of sweets for all
We all took the dog for a walk
But it sometimes took us
We took a ball and had a kick about
He got the best ice creams in the world
Then my mum would come to pick me up.

Michael Horrocks (13)
St Wilfrid's Catholic High School, Liverpool

My Nan

She carried it everywhere,
No matter if she was only going for a paper,
It was a big black bag,
When I was very little she would let me play with it,
Carrying it around making up stories.

The smell of her cooking filled the air,
As I walked up the path,
Hearing her sing along with the radio,
Always made me laugh.

One thing she loved,
Was the empty look of the betting shop,
She would pick her horses,
Hope they would win.

When I play cards,
I think of her putting down money
And saying, 'I can beat you any day.'
But she never did!

Kirsty Parkinson (13)
St Wilfrid's Catholic High School, Liverpool

The Magic Box
(Based on 'Magic Box' by Kit Wright)

In my magic box I would find . . .
A flying bird which would get me somewhere in 6.43 of a second
And I would carry a magic stopwatch
And a picture of my family,
A small fridge and cooker,
Cans and food and an alarm clock,
A magic football which would stick to my foot
Until you push a button so you can score a goal,
The Hulk and everlasting money.

Blayne Burgess (12)
St Wilfrid's Catholic High School, Liverpool

The World's Unfair

The world's not fair,
racists, evil,
terrorists, selfish.
The world's not fair
people can be cruel,
unkind, not care.

There should be more love
in this unfair world.
People die,
so unhappy people, feel they are important.
Children, men and women die
with no love.

The world's not fair,
people should respect each other,
love each other,
not kill.

People ruin their lives
for a bit of respect.
It's all unreal,
none of this matters.

Everyone's equal
don't you think?
Please think.

Natasha Clague (14)
St Wilfrid's Catholic High School, Liverpool

My Grandad John

Drip, drop, the melted chocolate dripped
His mouth watered
Drip, drop, the chocolate beckoned
A deep breath, a huge bite
His name was Grandad John

His nose shone out like the sun in the sky
'Give me more and more,' he said
The chocolate was tempting
So he shovelled it down
His name was Grandad John

Tick-tock, tick-tock
The great watch sounded
The sound of peace was music to my ears
He was sound asleep
Piled in a heap
His name was Grandad John

As the day was over
He would rise from his rest
He would hug us tight
That was my grandad all over
But in the end he is very missed
And now he's to rest in a better place
His name was Grandad John.

Mark Brehany (13)
St Wilfrid's Catholic High School, Liverpool

My Great Nan

Her name was Annie Rice,
The oldest person I knew,
She lived a long time,
Through World War I and II.

She always had a box of sweets,
That she kept in her room,
I remember her giving me some,
The toffee sticking to my teeth.

Her husband died after the war,
His name, Edward Rice,
He died of lung cancer,
A painful death.

She had five children,
May, Pat, Teddy, Billy and Charlie,
They miss their mother and father,
Though now they have their own children
And grandchildren.

She died on New Year's Eve,
The family weren't ready for her death,
We all still miss her loads,
But now she's in a better place.

Lauren Cannon (13)
St Wilfrid's Catholic High School, Liverpool

My Magical Tuck Box

My magical box has lots inside
I wish for my best friend to be there every day
A Christmas pressie or two
My very own fairy godparents to grant my wishes all day long
My mum's barley soup to smell all the time
Lots of money to buy what I want, like some pens to write to
my mother and father
My hamster, Nibbles, to stay with me everywhere I am
Some snow for Christmas so I could build a family of snowmen
Cartoons to watch whenever I want
Pictures of my family plus my friends to remember all the time
That's what will stay in my magical box.

Holley Murphy (12)
St Wilfrid's Catholic High School, Liverpool

My Grandad

The only thing he loved more than his chair was his pipes,
He had a whole rack full,
Out of all of them he loved his reddy-brown one most,
Every day you would see him cleaning his pipes,
With rainbow-coloured pipe cleaners,
Me and Grandma would make little men from them.

He would slowly fill it with tobacco from a green wallet,
Some days we would smoke together,
I had my own pipe (never filled),
At least once a day he would smoke,
As a small child I didn't like his pipe,
The tobacco juice would run into my mouth,
It tasted horrible.

Kane Sealeaf (13)
St Wilfrid's Catholic High School, Liverpool

Big Joe

We get lined up to warm ourselves,
His voice roars, rattling our eardrums,
'Red fence!'
We drop our heads, slowly moving like the seasons.

We return from our journey,
Our new coach stands there.
His eyes staring like a hawk,
The 6 foot 5 giant towers over us,
We shake at his feet,
This short-tempered legend bellows at us again.

Down we go to the floor,
'1, 2, 3, 4, 5, 6, 7, 8, 9, 10, get up.'
His voice echoes around the empty field.

Chris Oldfield (14)
St Wilfrid's Catholic High School, Liverpool

My Nanny Jean

My nan was a kind old lady,
She lived in an old persons' home,
I remember her room exactly
And the little red button too
We pushed it all the time
And every time a nurse came up
We pretended it wasn't us
We were much too small then
So we climbed upon the cupboard
And pushed the button then
But we jumped back off again
And sat on the bed as fast as we could
But the nurse always knew it was us.

Adam Law (13)
St Wilfrid's Catholic High School, Liverpool

He

His tattoos were memorable on his arm
But the rest of him was so calm
Stickmen, animals, black, blue
We all wonder, did he have a clue?

3 cars he had, all old and dusty,
Silver, black and red, were all rusty,
Car boot sale, that's where he was,
Driving around getting lost,
He would buy and sell,
Until the bell of 12 o'clock.

He'd drink and smoke every night,
When he drank, he would lose his sight,
The smoke would rise,
Up, up to my surprise,
Cautiously taking another puff,
Until he had had enough.

Zoe McKenna (13)
St Wilfrid's Catholic High School, Liverpool

Dreams

(Based on 'Magic Box' by Kit Wright)

In my magical box I would take my dad's 31-year-old
Gold shining ring, I would put it in my hand and curl my hand up
And make a wish that would light my whole life up,
It would come true, I would take my nana's and my grandpa's
Passport and say to myself, 'These are the faces that I never had
A chance to see.' I would also, at the end, take out a bunch of love
And friendship for everybody.

Leon Wiseman (12)
St Wilfrid's Catholic High School, Liverpool

Bluey

Full of life he was, as I remember him,
How much he loved to play, day and night,
Me and my sister around the garden all day,
Laughing and playing with him 'til dusk,
I hope he remembers me as I remember him.

I remember him small on Christmas Day,
I remember him cuddly, sleeping on my bed,
I also remember him at the vet's, just before he died,
It didn't hurt him, just a long sleep.

He was a good pet,
One of a kind,
He was my friend,
He was my dog.

Alex Whittle (13)
St Wilfrid's Catholic High School, Liverpool

The Mystery Box
(Based on 'Magic Box' by Kit Wright)

In my magic box I would find . . .
The fabulous pictures of my loving family
The comfiest bed which has the finest mattress
My family relaxing in the moonlight watching the years go by
The quality of Steven Gerrard and his amazing skills
My fairy cat having a fight with my dog
The greatest motorbike waiting to be revved around the streets
Everybody waiting for their roast dinner
The smell of a delightful bacon butty that my mum has cooked
That's what's in my magic box.

Jack McCluskie (12)
St Wilfrid's Catholic High School, Liverpool

My Magical Box
(Based on 'Magic Box' by Kit Wright)

In my magical box I would find . . .
The world's magical journal which goes with my never-ending story,
I would find my golden, barking dog which races out onto my pillow,
Not forgetting a picture of my family glowing in the background,
The smell of a brown bacon butty, keeping my eyes open as
                                        wide as an elephant,
A big open thick book that takes me into Never Never Land,
The sun that shines down onto the open seas
And definitely not forgetting my favourite DVDs taking me away
                                        into my favourite action movies
And I can't forget my favourite snacks of the day, crisps,
That is what will be in my box!

Gemma Hansen (12)
St Wilfrid's Catholic High School, Liverpool

My Magnificent Box
(Based on 'Magic Box' by Kit Wright)

In my magnificent box I would find . . .
A magical unicorn
All the tapes of WWE including Pay Per View Event
All my fantastic memories
A picture of my family
A picture of my favourite holiday
A time travel clock to travel to the good times
A magical feather for all my wishes
A warm bed for a thundery rainy night
The sound of the lapping blue sea on the soft, golden, sandy beach,
The soft sound of the children laughing at Christmas.

Julianah Fakolade (12)
St Wilfrid's Catholic High School, Liverpool

My Mystery Magic Box

(Based on 'Magic Box' by Kit Wright)

In my magical box I would find . . .
The very last unicorn
My grandfather's musical horn
A photo of my mum and dad
And also one of my big cousin
Who is very mad
A nice, warm bed
A big, soft brush for my tatty head
The smell of my best perfumes
A big CD player for my favourite tunes
The colour of the deep blue sea
And the soft sound of a buzzing bee
That is what I would put in my magic box.

Jessica Thorpe (12)
St Wilfrid's Catholic High School, Liverpool

My Magic Box

(Based on 'Magic Box' by Kit Wright)

In my magic box I would find . . .
The most warmest and comfortable quilt and pillow placed neatly into
the corner and bed socks too.
I would find the shining sunset blaring on the blue opening sea
with golden glittery sand.
On the other side of my box I would find . . .
The most yummy fudge cake with melted Flake on top.
Not forgetting a picture of me and my family on the happiest of days.

Danielle Gubb (12)
St Wilfrid's Catholic High School, Liverpool

Grandad

Grandad, the old light of my life
An ace soldier in his day

He loved to smoke cigars
A puff he took and blew it out
The smoke would linger around the room
Enjoying the taste of the strong aroma

Ol' Grandad had a passion for golf
Prize after prize he won
His shelves groaning with shiny, gold trophies

But Grandad sadly passed away
But good ol' Grandad is still remembered by Mum and me

Grandad's still remembered to this day
But we know his spirit will never fade away.

Christopher Brennan (14)
St Wilfrid's Catholic High School, Liverpool

My Magical Box
(Based on 'Magic Box' by Kit Wright)

In my magical box I would find . . .
A picture of my mum and family
The hottest hot chocolate ever
The biggest, lasting chocolate bar
And when I feel sad, I have my birthday and Christmas Day
The most magical money that never goes away
The smallest kitten the world has ever seen
The laughter of me and my friends
The smell of my mum's roast dinner on a Sunday afternoon
Now that's what's in my magical box.

Rachel Clear (12)
St Wilfrid's Catholic High School, Liverpool

My Magic Box

(Based on 'Magic Box' by Kit Wright)

In my magical box I would find . . .
Chocolate that would last forever,
My cosy bed on a cold winter's night,
Christmas morning to open all my presents,
The laugh of a 3-year-old playing in the sand,
My warm, cosy house,
All my friends to cheer me up,
The smell of a sausage butty on a Sunday morning,
The sound of my favourite song
And a picture of my family,
That's what I would have in my magic box.

Sarah Chialton (12)
St Wilfrid's Catholic High School, Liverpool

My Grandad

When my grandad smokes his pipe
A thick cloud of smoke bursts out,
Like a snake it slithers in the air,
It pollutes it with a poisonous smell,
But even though it smells so bad,
It reminds me of the smell of Grandad.

He keeps his false teeth in a glass full of water,
He keeps them on top of the toilet,
When they are clean enough,
He sticks them in his mouth,
He smiles at me then sings to me
And makes me feel very special.

Sarah Gardam (13)
St Wilfrid's Catholic High School, Liverpool

My Magical Box

(Based on 'Magic Box' by Kit Wright)

In my magical box I would have . . .
The new Wembley Stadium so I can play footy on it
One wish
A PlayStation 2
A dog to look after
A cake if I get hungry
Waking up to presents on Christmas
A football to play at Wembley
And football boots to play at Wembley.

Steven Milward (12)
St Wilfrid's Catholic High School, Liverpool

Three's The Record - Red Rum

My feet are fast,
My saddle red,
The fences are high,
They seem never-ending.

I'm in third now,
But second has fallen,
My master's whip stinging,
The finish line calling.

I'm catching up,
My feet are thunder,
Only a fence to go,
Three's the second.

I spring past first,
My master's rising,
My lead has increased,
The finish in sight.

I bow my head . . .
And then, the flashing.

Callum Johnstone (12)
Sacred Heart Catholic High School, Liverpool

Happiness Is . . .

Happiness is a flower
Of glowing pink
A brother or sister
Giving a wink
Happiness is the sun
That rises to its best
And then in the evening
Sets in the west
Happiness is the stars
Glinting in the night
In a mass of midnight-blue
They share out their twinkling light
Happiness is a shoal of tiny fish
Swimming a long way out to sea
A little laughing baby
Sitting contentedly on my knee
Happiness is the moon
Dazzling, glowing white
The clouds that float up in the sky
It's true they're soft and light
Happiness is a child's loving heart
That is as big as all of Rome
My family is happy
My family, my home.

Natalie J Romero (12)
Sacred Heart Catholic High School, Liverpool

The Day They Dropped The Bomb

(In response to work on nuclear war)

The burning flame coming
Towards our houses,
The pain and anger now coming from our houses.
The loud planes staggering down,
Splattering blood from every direction.
People dying.
Lots of people crying because they've lost their sons.
The brave soldiers went out to save their country.
God bless them.

Sean Seasman (13)
Sacred Heart Catholic High School, Liverpool

Me And Sean

We may not be bright
Or have a sensible life,
But we are best friends
And great minds think alike.

We play on our games,
Such as Timesplitters 2,
Fire-Warrior, Age of Empires
And The Sims too.

We play Warhammer
And Lord of the Rings,
We both like Blondie
And listen while she sings.

Sean's 11 months older than me,
Altogether,
We'll be best friends
Forever and ever.

Jack Cartwright (11)
Sale Grammar School, Sale

Throughout The World

Throughout the world,
Russia
Children dying, suffering,
Imagine if it were you,
Suddenly death, hostages
And you were in the centre,
Think.

Throughout the world,
Africa,
Drought, hunger,
No food, no water,
Homes made out of mud
And you lived like that,
Think.

Throughout the world,
Saudi Arabia,
Polluted cities,
Dirty water, poisoned food,
Barefooted twenty-four hours
And you live like that,
Think.

Thomas Powell (12)
Sale Grammar School, Sale

The Scared

My heart was thumping like mad,
I felt so, so sad.
My hand felt so numb,
I said to myself,
'Don't do that, don't be so dumb.'
I got the sword in my hand
And hoped for this land;
How I would kill to be alive again.

Stephanie Hong (11)
Sale Grammar School, Sale

Flight Over Manchester

Hovering above Manchester at night,
Looking below at the artificial light,
Watching the multicoloured cars go by and by,
In my helicopter in the sky.

Men and women going to pubs,
Young couples going to nightclubs,
I see flats with windows of white,
In my helicopter flight at night.

Buildings below like all the types of square,
As I go past I stop and stare,
At everything around me,
From my helicopter a lot I can see.

Cars passing below,
With lights as white as snow,
Above a plane passes,
Dropping fuel that looks like gasses.

I have seen all these things above and below,
I have seen enough so now I must go,
Past the Trafford Centre's big dome,
In my helicopter bound for home.

Adam Legg (11)
Sale Grammar School, Sale

The President's Mind

My mind is spoken
War will break out
Peace time has been broken
We will fight day and night
They shall feel our fright
Our armies will seek weapons of destruction
Ending this time of sad interruption
Afterwards will we be sad
For the people of Baghdad?
Perhaps the President's mind will?

Andrew Carson (11)
Sale Grammar School, Sale

Autumn

The rustle and bustle of falling leaves
The swishing and swaying of on-looking trees
The skittering and scattering of skinny red squirrels
Round and round they turn and twirl

The birds, which are chirping way up in their nests
The hedgehogs and badgers getting ready to rest
The foxes that come out of their dens at night
The owls that hoot and wait to take flight

The changing of colour from green to brown
The lights go on early all round the town
The conkers and pine cones that cover the floor
The warmness has gone so we're chilled to the core

And now as we wait 'til the winter takes hold
We'll marvel in awe, as nature is unfurled
The magic of autumn is a wonderful sight
We can't underestimate it though, try as we might.

Calum Clarke (13)
Sale Grammar School, Sale

Blaze

A blaze is growing in the storm,
Like the two ways which lightning and thunder are torn,
The blaze awakens, the fire spreads,
All plants and leaves left for dead,
Struck by lightning, the trees fall to the ground,
Toppling over into a huge mound,
The thunder tries to warn the animals to go back home,
But the trees are destroyed there, on their own,
The rain reaches the ground, the fire is dimmed,
The wind comes and blows out the fire, this is a strange whim,
The wind keeps on going, it blows away all the despair,
The ruins stand there,
Still the air.

Ben Stokes (11)
Sale Grammar School, Sale

Migration

As I soared above the craggy tarn,
I dreamt about my dry warm barn,
Heading south I must go,
The wind and the rain they were my foe.

Out across the sea so wide,
With my companion by my side,
We flew and flew such a long way,
Until at last we reached Montana Bay.

We were greeted by a colourful tern,
Who popped his head through a green fern.
He opened his beak and quacked 'Hello,'
Thank goodness here there is no snow.

Enjoying the warmth of the everyday sun,
My friend and I had so much fun.
As spring approached I returned to my barn
And once again I flew over that familiar tarn.

Jack Marsland (11)
Sale Grammar School, Sale

Daydreaming

D oes your mind wander
A nd your imagination take over?
Y ou've got your head in the clouds
D reaming of other things,
R eality disappears and you're . . .
E verywhere but not here.
A nother place, another time,
M aking up stories,
I nventing a fantasy world, *stop!*
N o more roaming,
G et back to reality.

Olivia Al-Noah (11)
Sale Grammar School, Sale

Creature Teacher!

It was an ordinary day in the classroom,
Miss Jones was marking my book.
She suddenly stopped and gurgled
And gave me an alien look!

Green slimy tentacles burst from her skin
And she started to shiver and shake,
Next thing I knew, she was dancing
Like Justin Timberlake!

She gobbled up last night's homework
And smashed up the tables and chairs,
Then went and demolished the blackboard,
Whilst we all made a dash for the stairs!

'Aaarrrggghhh!'
Cried the panicking children,
Who were running down the hall.
'There's a monster right behind you,
Don't just stand there and stall!'

I turned and was slimed by my teacher
And fell backwards onto the floor,
Then quickly got up to make my escape,
Out of the main entrance door!

A loud roaring noise rose behind me
And I fell to my knees once more,
The school turned into a spaceship
And into the sky it soared!

Now all I have is the nightmares,
This dripping green slime on my face
And the memories of my creature teacher,
Who blasted off into space!

Charlotte Lamb (11)
Sale Grammar School, Sale

The Four Seasons

Spring,
A season of new beginnings.
Sun's starting to come out,
Trees and flowers waking up,
Newborn animals see the world,
A season of new beginnings.
Summer,
A season of fun and games,
Fruit ripening,
Everyone relaxing,
Children playing,
Clear blue sky,
A season of fun and games.
Autumn,
A season of sleep and colour,
Animals hibernating,
Trees lose their leaves,
Red, gold and brown,
A season of sleep and colour.
Winter,
A season of love and beauty,
Snow falling,
˙ Ice freezing,
Families celebrating,
Everyone smiling,
A season of love and beauty.

Beth Aulton (12)
Sale Grammar School, Sale

The Day My House Went Crazy!

The day my house went crazy,
My dad hit his head on the wall,
My brother grew really tall,
My mum hung from the door
And I fell through the floor.

The day my house went crazy,
I hid in the bathroom,
The longer I stayed, the more it became a tomb,
First the loo shouted, 'Boo'
Then flushed away my shoe.

The day my house went crazy,
The humour carried into the hall,
Pictures started dancing on the wall,
I played some music and the stairs began to move,
They swayed to and fro along with *groove*.

The day my house went crazy,
The craziness carried into the kitchen,
My mother was a-stitchin',
Knives and forks jumped out of drawers,
As me and my brother had food wars.

The day my house went crazy,
Up it went to the bedroom,
It was my bedtime soon,
The pillows danced upon the bed,
As teddies leapt onto my head.

The day my house went crazy,
The day was drawing to an end,
The house started to amend,
Everything stepped back in line,
As the clock at twelve began to chime.

Andrew Wilson (12)
Sale Grammar School, Sale

A Sorting Hat's Song

I'm unlike average, common hats,
I'm actually more lonely,
There is no other hat you'll match,
With me, I'm one and only,
I can put you into Slytherin,
If you're vicious and you're cunning
And like to have what's good for you,
You're ambitious and you're stunning,
I can put you into Gryffindor,
If you're fearless and you're brave,
Boldest of the houses four,
Shall seek honour 'til the grave!
I can put you into Ravenclaw,
If you are sharp and you're wily,
More intelligent than ever before,
Successful and respected highly,
I can put you into Hufflepuff,
If you're just and you're sincere,
Much more than simply loyal enough,
For the whole of the school year,
I have never been mistaken,
Because I am always right
And to whichever house you're taken,
Don't get into a fright,
In the yearly competitions,
We shall soon see who can win
And the duelling and the Quidditch,
All shall now begin!

Aisha Baden (11)
Sale Grammar School, Sale

On Top Of Blackpool Tower

I love it up here
I can see further
Than the pier

The sight is so nice
Though the weather
Is as cold as ice

You can see for miles
It feels like I can see
The whole of the British Isles

I can see some cars
They seem so far
As far as Mars

I feel so high
Like I have been launched
Right into the sky.

Sophie Wheeler (12)
Sale Grammar School, Sale

Great Minds

G eniuses in their own right
R evolutionary ideas
E qual to Einstein
A rithmetic master
T echnological thinkers

M asterminds
I ntelligent as elephants
N obel Prize winners
D ynamic designers
S uperior intellects.

Ben Hughes (11)
Sale Grammar School, Sale

Trees

As I wandered down the lane,
I had to stop and stare.
The sun was setting in the distance,
A vision so rare.

Its orange, red and yellow rays
Shining through the trees.
Setting a stage so beautiful,
I fell to my knees.

The wind was whistling through the leaves,
The trees danced to its tune,
Side to side, back and forth,
Finally bowing to the moon.

As it was now getting dark,
I carried on down the lane.
A memory to cherish,
Would I ever be the same?

Michael Savage (12)
Sale Grammar School, Sale

Chocolate

C hunky bars too hard to bite
H ot as a soothing drink
O ozing out the wrapper on a boiling hot day
C runchy on a chocolate cake
O range flavoured for a change
L uscious truffles that melt in your mouth
A lmond to change the texture
T asty as a treat
E xtra large for extra pleasure!

Andrew Aylott (11)
Sale Grammar School, Sale

Missing

The wind whistles through the trees
And the sunlight marches on the dancing leaves,
Over hill and under dale,
Wherever my heart says *go*, I will not fail.

Even if I walk a thousand miles,
Through the seas and over stiles,
Whispering like a spider's web,
Each step fearless I will tread.

The sunrise is bright and the air is cool,
I see the shadow of you through the gloom,
Your smile gleams through the fragile night,
Your voice like a lullaby all alight.

Wandering aimlessly through the trees,
Your presence seems to follow me,
I stare up to the bright blue sky
And watch the clouds go floating by.

With a trance I watch you go,
Through the trees and mist you flow,
In my thoughts and in my dreams,
Rolling down the tumbling streams.

I picture you still here with me,
Months have passed yet still I see,
The hope that I stay in your mind,
Until, one day, you seek and find.

Through delicate winter I stare and hope,
That spring will come and fingers grope,
Till summer comes triumphant bright,
Through the darkness and the night.

No voice pounding quiet in my head,
No trail of where I should be led,
No eyes staring out like sapphires in the sky,
But I'll wait for you until I fall and die.

The grass still whispers of a silent shadow,
The wind has wiped it small and narrow,
Yet memory will still prevail
And then my heart will call and hail . . .

Sarah Turner (13)
Sale Grammar School, Sale

Waves

There are waves that splish
There are waves that splash
There are waves that pound
There are waves that crash

There are waves that destroy
There are waves that flood
There are waves that enjoy
There are waves that are good

There are waves in the ocean
There are waves in the sea
There are waves that cause commotion
There are waves that make harmony

There are waves for surfing
There are waves for sailing
There are waves for swimming
There are waves for drowning

There are gentle waves
There are soft waves
There are towering waves
There are powerful waves

What a wonderful world of waves we have!

Nicholas Bell (11)
Sale Grammar School, Sale

Darkness

A cold, bloody silence illuminating all sound
A black, steel-sharp claw scratching your spine
A dark, red-eyed eagle gnawing at your neck
A silent wind whispering in your ear
The air you breathe stops stone cold in your throat
Your limbs are numb and decaying from fear
Your eyes feel like they have been pulled out of their sockets
Your fingers tremble like an ever-going tambourine
You feel your heart will rip out from your chest from beating
A chilling cold feeling is climbing up your spine
The hairs on your neck are prickling like a hedgehog
You feel an army of ants crawling up your spine
Your stomach lurches like a butterfly in a ball
You feel like your bones have been ground to jelly
Your eyes are jerky like a ball on a loose string
Your body trembles, your face is pale
There is an echo of a blood-cold scream
You feel a sharp cold blade cutting through your neck
And an echo . . . an echo of a blood-cold scream.

Mohamed Zardab (11)
Sale Grammar School, Sale

Great Minds

Great minds think alike,
Fools seldom differ.

Is this true or is it not?
Was Einstein bright or a bit of a clot?

The same with Newton, whose brain was sound,
Discovered gravity by an apple falling to the ground.

Stephen Hawkins is a bright guy,
He deals with physics like it's as easy as Pie.

But my favourite great mind is Homer - not the Olympian,
Rather Homer, the greatest American (Simpson).

Jonathan Clarke (11)
Sale Grammar School, Sale

In The London Eye

High in the sky I'm in the London Eye,
High in the sky I see the Abbey and Tower,
High in the sky I can see the Palace,
These are all architectural wonders that only I can see.

High in the sky I look down on creation,
High in the sky those people look like ants,
High in the sky all the cars move like flies,
Everything is so small when I'm high in the sky.

High in the sky I almost see until the end of the Earth,
High in the sky I see a patchwork of parks and fields,
High in the sky I see the rolling River Thames,
Those boats seem not to move, when you're so high in the sky.

High in the sky everything appears so small,
Whereas down on the ground that's not the case at all!
When I'm back on the ground it's me who's so small.

Craig Kitchener (11)
Sale Grammar School, Sale

Winter

It's here again bringing colds, wheezes, flu and sneezes,
Endless rain racing towards the ground,
Pirouetting and dancing as it rebounds,
Wind that whips the leaves off trees
And blows so strong it makes you freeze,
Children play in hats, coats, scarves and mitts,
In gardens which lack any colourful bits,
Darkness follows you home from school,
No playing out or playing the fool,
Stay inside, cosy fire, watch TV, wile away the hours,
Thick clouds hide a cold moon glow,
Next morning awaken to a blanket of snow,
Christmas soon, a tree and lights, presents make the cold alright.

Charlotte Mapp (11)
Sale Grammar School, Sale

Autumn Is Here

Hanging on by no more than a thread
Frightened to look down
The spotted leaves sway in the wind
Many have fallen to their death
Only few remain!

These creatures are harmless
They are all proven innocent
Those of yellow ochre say their goodbyes
Whereas the burnt umbers can only watch and pray
Will both families survive?

Now we come to the last few days of the season
Have the strong winds defeated the leaves?
There is silence in the forests
What could this mean?
Oh, there they are
What a sad sight.

Daniel Fisher (11)
Sale Grammar School, Sale

Autumn!

Autumn is here and the trees are almost bare.
The leaves are falling beneath my feet.
Brown, orange, green and gold,
Are the colours that cover the ground.
I am alone, but I still hear noise.
The noise of leaves crinkling and crunching.
Now it's raining, I'd better be careful,
The leaves are slippery and dangerous,
I find another conker to add to my collection,
Autumn is now over and winter has begun.

Bethany Cooper (11)
Sale Grammar School, Sale

Great Minds

They have thoughts like miracles and ideas like dreams,
They have thoughts that flow like rivers and streams.
They take over you with their creation,
Doing the same to the whole of the nation.

They give us a picture of their intellect,
Just like the person who invented the Internet.
They toil like worker ants,
Struggling not by chance.

They show us reason
And help us with our maths,
They commit treason
And are sometimes very daft.

They make us our own mastermind
And give us lots of tips,
They aren't just found in human kind,
They're also found in ferrets.

Michael Hopkins (11)
Sale Grammar School, Sale

Autumn

The sun is low in the sky,
A conker fell and caught my eye.
The leaves are now turning brown
And ready to start fluttering down.
The squirrel burying his collection
And guarding them, with protection.
There is one animal fast asleep,
But nothing is heard from it, not a peep.
The elegant robin chirping a tune,
But unfortunately the sun will be setting soon.
Autumn is a great time of year
And now we know that winter is near!

Kara Wilson (11)
Sale Grammar School, Sale

As I Walk Home From School

As I walk home from school
The faces flow past me in a blur
The chat fills my head and blocks out my thoughts

All I can see is the lollipop man's smiling face
All I hear are the screams and shouts of children
Running to their friends, telling them what a great day they've had

I hear a call above the babble
It's my best friend waving vigorously
Shouting that she'll see me tomorrow

I step into the road but a car zooms past unexpectedly
Quickly I withdraw my foot then
I see a space in the traffic and run across

The pavement ahead of me is strung with children
Laughing and joking as they wait
For the bus to come and take them home

The bus arrives with the driver's blank and thoughtless face
Children file on, pay, then run to grab the seat by the window
Fumes choke me but when I look up the bus has gone, the children
with it

I see my house
Just 100 yards away
But I walk, not enough energy to run

Little tornadoes of leaves
Brush past my feet
As I unlock the door

I'm home

At last.

Jenny Brocklebank (11)
Sale Grammar School, Sale

Because We Humans Are So Cruel

The sounds and smells in the cold desolate air,
Far too much for us all to bear,
The nerves were building in the men tonight,
Not knowing whether they were going to die or freeze of fright,
The whistles blew as the men went hurdling over,
The great trench walls when the guns started firing and
                                        mines exploding,
The cold wind in the air was like shrapnel to their faces,
Mixed with the rain and the mud in some cases,
The spirit of hope was not to be,
Men stumbled down dead, some younger than twenty,
It was a horrific sight, that blood-fuelled act of rage,
It was a massacre that should have been encaged,
But if you made it there and back and survived,
Then you could live and bless every day alive,
It wasn't just bullets that killed, it was grenades and gas bombs too,
'The blast is far too great,' they told us, 'it would rupture your insides.'
Just imagine the pain and agony you'd go through if you stayed alive,
So aren't you glad in this day and age you weren't a part of that?
Imagine the hell those men had to go through, that you
                                        have to respect,
So spare a thought after you've read this, for those who lost their lives,
And their innocent families, some men even had children and wives,
What some may even ask is why it ever started at all
And to that you may reply, because we humans are so cruel.

David Ciaramella (13)
Sale Grammar School, Sale

Autumn

Autumn is a beautifully colourful season,
Everywhere is decorated lovely with red,
Yellow, orange and brown.

Autumn is a greeting season,
Greeting people with falling down colourful leaves
And rice bowing their head.

Autumn is a bright and cheery season,
Cheering everyone like cheerleaders,
Swinging colourful leaves with a nice soft wind.

Autumn is a busy season,
People harvesting their food for winter,
Animals collecting their food for winter.

Autumn is a very full season,
Fully coloured leaves and trees,
People are fully fed and so are animals.

Autumn, there is no such beautiful season as autumn,
Autumn, the nice, beautiful, colourful and cheering season.

Yoorim Lee (11)
Sale Grammar School, Sale

Great Minds

Our minds are capable of many things,
Like composing, reflecting and, I suppose,
That of all the thoughts inside my mind,
The greatest wish is peace to mankind.

The world is such an upsetting place,
At times we cause a real disgrace.
But with good thoughts becoming reality,
Our world will gain from positivity.

Emily Frier (11)
Sale Grammar School, Sale

Seasons Of The Year

The sky is bright, cloudy but clear,
Animals are born, plants reappear,
Grass re-grows at this time of year,
The first season, spring, is here.

The sun is out, all through the day,
All the children run out to play,
All the adults playing croquet,
The second season, summer, is on display.

Golden leaves, orange and brown,
The wind picks up as they dance around.
Little brown conkers falling down,
The third season, autumn, comes round.

When skies go grey and white,
The frost begins overnight.
When robins begin to make their flight,
The fourth season, winter, is in sight.

Georgina Sawyer (11)
Sale Grammar School, Sale

A Boy Called Frank

I once knew a boy called Frank,
He was in the army,
He had a number one rank.

Frank had a mate called Davy,
He was a great guy,
He was always sailing away in the navy.

Frank and Davy also had a mate called Steve,
He was in the air force,
So they could only get together on leave.

Jonathan Hardy (11)
Sale Grammar School, Sale

In A Hot Air Balloon

In a hot air balloon,
I can see
A field full of sheep like
Cotton buds on a green carpet.

Way up high in a basket,
I can see,
Cows in a field like
Ping-pong balls on a table tennis surface.

In a hot air balloon,
I can see,
Yellow and black taxis,
Looking like bumblebees.

High in my basket,
I can touch,
Clouds like,
Candyfloss I'd buy at the fair.

I'd like to stay here,
In my Legoland world,
But back to reality I must go,
As this poem is due in tomorrow.

Jenny Baker (11)
Sale Grammar School, Sale

Limerick

I have a friend called Dandy,
Whose hair could be described as sandy,
She runs on four legs,
Sits up and begs,
To have a dog as a friend is quite handy.

Sam Stoddart (11)
Sale Grammar School, Sale

A Snow-Capped Poem

A snow-capped heaven,
A mile-high dream,
Dozens of mountains,
So beautiful it seems.

Planes pass below me,
Like I'm above the sky,
To me they look no more
Than small white dragonflies.

If the Earth were a room,
My head would touch the ceiling,
I hope the wallpaper of this planet
Never decides to start peeling.

I realised then I was on top of the clouds;
The shock of this made me laugh out loud,
I though it would be tall but not as tall as this,
Where was I? You ask
On Mt Everest.

Wolfie McFarlane (11)
Sale Grammar School, Sale

The Boxer

I am a merry boxer
I get into the ring
Wallop, wallop, thud I go
Until the bell goes ding
When the bell goes ding again
I go back to my stool
And stare at my opponent
The ugly little fool
Ding, there goes the bell again
I rush back to my bout,
Wallop, wallop, thud, blad, 'Oww!'
'Nine, ten, *out!'*

Lauren McIntosh (11)
Sale Grammar School, Sale

The Picture

Outside the picture, no tone sings its God -
Given note, stillness paralyses the desolate panorama, nothing lives,
Why are these simple pieces of artistic expression doomed to an
everlasting fate?
The expressionless victim hangs pleadingly, like a crook's last breath
at the gallows.
Dust smothers the surface like tears, tears of the once dignified king of
his long forgotten empire.

Inside the picture, the sun fails to come.
The rain has come, but no drop is yet to kiss the floor.
The innocent people come, but never go.
The world is still . . . resting . . . dying . . .
Raindrops stop in mid-fall, no feeling . . . no pain . . . no emotion . . .
A fly breathes no breath, but lives, the frail, intricate wings moistened
with the essence of raindrops, glisten in mid-flutter.
A trickle of rain freezes on a windowpane. Emotionless . . .
expressionless . . . lifeless.

I am that picture. My dreams are false. They do not exist in the torture
called life I know. I do not have a life and never will do.
I am doomed to exist only in pain and suffering,
to hang from a wall forbidding movement and life. Life or death,
I wish for one of them.
I live in the middle.

Sam Rankin (11)
Sale Grammar School, Sale

The World Today

An old man walking down the street,
Wandering, staring at his feet,
Thinking what had gone so wrong,
From the time when he was young,
He remembered a day when, not like now,
You wouldn't step in half-eaten chow,
People would be filled with amazing cheer
And when they met they would not sneer,
Neighbours were friendly, would nod and wave,
Unlike today, when you meet, you rave,
Children would not complain that they were bored
And they would not spit chewing gum on the floor,
For their elders they would have some respect,
But now with their parents they will not connect,
They used to help the disabled across the street,
Now they won't help anyone they meet,
The floor should not be littered with junk,
It should be in a garbage truck,
The children would help to water the flowers,
Now they sit around moaning for hours,
People used to have fun playing marbles by the house,
Now people have fun watching TV on the couch,
'A miracle of science,' some people say,
I think that 'science' should call it a day.

Elizabeth Evans (12)
Sale Grammar School, Sale

Looking From The CN Tower

Starts with a queue,
It takes only a minute to get to the top,
But in the end,
Oh what a view.

Looking straight down,
I can see the Sky Dome,
It's the stadium where the Blue Jays baseball team
Call home.

Looking across the city, the sun went down,
Although the sky was dark,
You could see thousands of lights
Twinkling like stars.

Looking down on streams
Of traffic,
The lights of the cars like huge rivers,
One flowed white,
The other flowed red.

In a special viewing area,
Where you can look around some more,
This doesn't sound scary,
But it had a glass floor,

Looking down
At my feet,
I seemed to be hovering
Above the pavements,
Many hundreds of feet.

Ryan Sweetman (11)
Sale Grammar School, Sale

What Is It?

It's got green hair
and two pairs of ears.
It's as big as a bear.
It's pulled me out of my chair
and now it's chasing me down the stairs.

It's got sharp teeth
and these huge webbed feet.
It's blue on top and purple underneath.
I think it wants something to eat
and it's dragging me out of our street.

It's got scaly toes,
a belly button that glows,
there's fire dripping from its nose.
What? Fangs? It's got hundreds of those
and it's hurrying me over these unlit roads.

It's got slippery skin,
bulging eyes and luminous veins,
its fingers grip like freezing chains.
Oh no, I think we're off again
and it's rushing me along this winding lane.

It's okay, I'm free
and I think that maybe
I'd better say this very quietly
because it was, after all, you see,
just my own imagination running away with me.

Daniel Scanlon (11)
Sale Grammar School, Sale

Pets Or Property?

In this crazy world where violence rules,
Why are animals treated like fools?
They love you, help you, guide you,
But still are hurled aside.

What has an animal ever done wrong?
To be left outside alone so long.
An animal's a loyal friend,
Not just a Christmas gift.

Why do they deserve to be left chained
And always greatly pained?
No chance of fun and games
At the end of a piece of rope.

An animal should be loved and fed
And have a nice warm bed,
Not a cold, damp hutch outside,
Or a tiny room downstairs.

You can see it in their eyes
And hear it in their tearful sighs,
That while you are sat at home,
The animal wants to roam.

Christian Greenstreet (13)
Sale Grammar School, Sale

A Great Mind

A great mind is like an open door,
Allowing things to drift in,
A tornado of information,
Faithful and reliable,
Picking up as it goes along,
There is no stopping a great mind,
Sometimes it's as sharp as a blade,
Sometimes it's as slow as a tortoise,
A true great mind never stops going!

Daniel Stone (12)
Sale Grammar School, Sale

The Siren

There goes the siren that warns of the air raid
There are the screams of the innocent civilians
Run to the spitfires and get ready to attack them
Hurry up men! Run! There's no time to waste

Remove all the wheel blocks and get in the cockpits
Start up the engines; fight off the attackers
Zoom down the runway, we've got to get airborne
Got to fight off the Germans before it's too late

Rolling, turning, diving, I can't shake them off
I take a direct hit and fall towards the ground
Eject and activate your parachute
Land on the ground, knowing you've failed

Sitting there watching, with great sorrow
Watching the Germans bomb our base
Watching your friends fighting just the way you did
Just to get shot down, just the way you did
The Germans have won this battle, but we'll win the war.

Lee Horsefield (13)
Sale Grammar School, Sale

Autumn Has Arrived

It's that time of year again
Where the weather seems to change
The days turn dull and the night goes dark

Wind is blowing in your face
Rain is splashing at your feet
Conkers crack upon your head

Out come your coats
Away goes your bikini
Sandals get swapped for boots

No one really enjoys it
But no one really complains
Autumn has arrived and everyone knows it.

Emily Rothwell (13)
Sale Grammar School, Sale

View From Above

I'm on top of a mountain overlooking Vienna
I can see small cars like bees
Buzzing about in their hive

The impressive River Danube meanders its way
Far into the distance
As if cutting the city in two

The bridges that glistened in the sun
Were the only connection to the other side
It made me think how long they took to build

The vineyards stretching down below
Were a carpet of green against the blue sky
Reminded me of a painting on a wall

The church spires soared high into the sky
Way above the many buildings
And busy roads.

Matthew Church (11)
Sale Grammar School, Sale

Snow

The morning comes
The curtains are drawn
The room lights up by the glow of the snow
Looking out the window
No ground can be seen
Car windows glisten as the sun rises
Children play wearing hats, gloves and scarves
They run around with cold red noses
As the day goes on, the sky gets darker
When night falls in, the streets are empty
And then you see lights being switched off, one by one
Then all you can hear is silence.

Zeynab Mohajeri (11)
Sale Grammar School, Sale

On The Top Of The Empire State Building

I am so high up in the air,
With plenty of breath to spare,
I look down on NY City,
On my own, what a pity.

Yellow blobs race around,
Tiny black specks make plenty of sound,
Skyscrapers stand o' so tall,
Neighbouring the busy mall.

NY High School is motionless up here,
I bet the bar is selling beer,
Houses begin to light up because of night,
Black specks notice moonlight.

Newspaper boys begin to clear,
As night draws near,
Motels and drive-in movies are loud and clear,
O' what a view it is up here.

Thomas Higham (11)
Sale Grammar School, Sale

High In The Sky In My Big Red Balloon

High in the sky I ascend to the clouds
High in the sky above I see blue
High in the sky I look down on creation

High in the sky I see beetle-like cars
High in the sky I see relentless sea waters
High in the sky I see scurrying ant people
High in the sky I see city lights gleaming

High in the sky I hear the wind speaking
Down below all is in chaos
High in the sky is where I long to be.

Philip Grubert (11)
Sale Grammar School, Sale

Damilola

Damilola was a normal boy, but when walking home from school,
He was feeling quite confused by the boys who were so cruel,
They laughed at him and called him names, things he didn't
understand,
He never did a thing to them, yet was still bullied by this gang.

Damilola lived in South London, in the toughest council estate,
He shared this with his family and near this home he met his fate,
They had moved there from Nigeria, to give him a better life,
But this life was soon to be taken, by some attackers and a knife.

Damilola was a happy boy, but when walking home from school,
He was feeling so afraid, of the group that were so cruel,
They were chasing him and scaring him, things were getting out of
hand,
In a council block, so close to home, his body came to land.

Frightened and alone, he fell down to the ground,
He felt the pain shoot through him and then no life was to be found.

Damilola just wanted to be happy and make some newfound friends,
Why did that short life of his have to come to such an end?
As he lay and felt the pain, he wondered what he had done wrong,
He was always nice to everyone and he hadn't lived here that long!

Damilola's parents felt so full of grief, what could they do?
They'd always cared and loved their son and now his life was through,
Who could be so heartless? So cruel and so insane,
To hurt their son in such a way, that they'd never see him again.

Damilola did not deserve it, he was just an innocent boy,
He wanted a life of laughter, of success and filled with joy,
So who would want to take this laughter, take away all this?
And leave behind the pain, of losing a life we now all miss.

Damilola.

Sarah Medley (13)
Sale Grammar School, Sale

The City

Up from above

The city was dark and gloomy, fumes flooded the air,
Shops were like pockets with a zip here and there!

Up from above

Umbrellas were like daisies dancing in the rain,
Small ant-like creatures scurried down the lane.

Up from above

The roads were sharp and twisty, like a bullet from a gun
Everything was getting clearer, my journey was now
Done!

Rachael Kettle (11)
Sale Grammar School, Sale

The Tiger

It strolls around the rainforest,
It ponders along in snow,
It can travel very fast
And also travel slow.

A solitarily animal,
Often it's seen alone,
A beautiful animal
Which nobody can own.

It's an expert hunter,
Its strength is there to see,
It can tackle any animal,
Whilst others run and flee.

Its colours so recognisable,
Its stripes so clear and bold,
Its beauty is a wonder,
Its species is so old.

Ralph Taylor (13)
Sale Grammar School, Sale

Under The Mountain

Under the mountain there are small and big trees,
Under the mountain there are patchwork fields,
Under the mountain there are buzzing bees,
Under the mountain there is a knight with a shield.

Under the mountain there are still roads,
Under the mountain there are multicoloured cars,
Under the mountain there are miniscule toads,
Under the mountain there is a crashing car.

Under the mountain there are tiny people,
Under the mountain there are square buildings,
Under the mountain there are church steeples,
Under the mountain there is a church.

Alex Bretten (12)
Sale Grammar School, Sale

From Atop This Hill I Can See

From atop of this hill I can see,
Little people as big as ants,
Also there is taxis and cars like little bumblebees,
Lots of things I can see.

From atop of this hill I can see,
A field like a big green sea,
Also a plant that I think is a tree,
Lots of things I can see.

From atop of this hill I can see,
A river like strands of cotton,
Also a bus like a little yellow square,
Lots of things I can see . . .

Atop this hill.

Jack Wetherell (11)
Sale Grammar School, Sale

Looking Down From Above

You're in a tree in a rainforest you can look down,
You see things on the faraway ground,
Sitting on a branch, you're so tall,
Things on the ground look very, very small.

Focus on a monkey like a small brown bee,
Buzzing round from tree to tree,
All the other animals look like ants,
Or small black beetles doing a dance.

Big bushes and shrubs look like moss,
Your tree really shows them who's boss,
Climb up higher all you can see is,
Tree after tree after tree after tree.

You look back down now you're *really* tall
Then the branch breaks, you begin to fall
Ouch! That hurt!

Lucy Rowney (11)
Sale Grammar School, Sale

Bird's Eye View

I could see cities
With ants as people
And buildings like mazes

I could see green fields
With similar shapes and sizes
And different shades of colour

I could see snow-capped mountains
That looked like bumps in the road
A giant car would pass

I could see life on a whole different level
Where I was sitting
In the back of a JMC plane!

Rachel Savill (11)
Sale Grammar School, Sale

The Impenetrable Jungle

Yet again I am stepping into the impenetrable jungle,
In search of my long-lost treasures.
I step straight into the dimly lit forest,
Determined to return with the riches I seek.

As I walk I can feel the floor,
Carpeted with exotic flowers and lush greenery.
I place my foot down on the hide of a peculiar beast,
Lying motionless across the matted forest.

Things cling to my ankles as I walk,
They remind me of skins shed by slithering snakes.
Abandoned garments no longer required,
I dare not look down.

Wooden structures loom above my head,
Hiding animals and birds of every colour and shape.
Animals and flowers border me in,
Making me feel claustrophobic.

Fantastic creatures fly across my horizon,
Defying every law of gravity.
The eyes of big cats are fixed on me,
From their perches, ready to pounce.

The ceiling-like canopy, clad with creeping,
Clinging, cascading vines.
Scuttling insects peer out from dry,
Dark corners, making it impossible to relax.

The silence is broken by the throb of drums
And native voices wailing.
Then there I see my one true treasure,
I grab my purse and sort out my money.

'Lydia! Turn that racket off and tidy your room!'
'Mum, I can't. I'm going out, I'll be back for tea!' I reply.
I turn my CD player off
And leave my room and my jungle behind.

Lydia Gaunt (13)
Sale Grammar School, Sale

The Ride

I wake up and I look
At the calendar on my wall
And I can't believe it's taken
So long to arrive
I've been waiting for weeks
For today
We get in the car
And drive very far
Away
To the ride today
I'm so excited
To be here
And to go on the ride
I rush out the car
Straight to the ride
Everyone's been talking about it
Sounds so great
Looks so great
Wonderful and bright
I'm in the queue
And I need the loo
But I'm nearly at the front now
So I stay
I'm on the ride
It's going slowly fast
But strangely it doesn't feel right
It's quite boring actually
It turns out waiting
Was the best part of the ride.

Sian Llewelyn (12)
Sale Grammar School, Sale

The Statue Of Liberty

On the Statue of Liberty looking down
Bobbing boats as far as the eye
Can see

Yellow taxis dotted here and there
The honking horns and screeching sirens
People scurrying like ants

The hustle and bustle
Of rush hour traffic down below
And I'm up here peaceful watching birds fly by

Now it's the end of my stay
Just a small bite out of the
Big Apple.

Richard Smith (11)
Sale Grammar School, Sale

Minds

So many minds in this world
And none of them think the same

So many broken hearts are found
Deep down inside

So much love in the air
Enough for a world to share

So many dreams in people's heads
Waiting to come true

All of them wait in the air
Waiting to come down to you.

Nigel Suchoparek (13)
Sale Grammar School, Sale

Looking From A Cloud!

From a cloud I see the Earth,
A green carpet field,
Almost completely covered in cotton bud sheep,
A closer look shows me the blood,
The red on their fluffy body,
The sight of no movement,
Breaks my heart into a million pieces.

From a cloud I see the Earth,
A brown scribble fence from a young person,
Like a wiggly line on the floor,
It wiggles and jiggles,
It turns to make odd patterns,
The sight of no movement,
Breaks my heart into a million pieces.

Gemma Grime (11)
Sale Grammar School, Sale

In A Cave Of Wonder

As I was floating around,
In a boat as small as an ant,
The thing I saw above me was
A dark brown cave.
It had a rough surface,
It looked like nobody had discovered
This cave for a long time,
There was red and yellow,
Lots of pictures of mammals
And on one,
There were people smiling,
I realised I had discovered,
It was a cave of the Stone Age!

Kate Berry (12)
Sale Grammar School, Sale

Hope

We all think our lives are bad
That we have nothing good to live for
We slump around acting sad
Thinking that we're poor
The ones who strain every day
Are the people who just don't moan
They work their lives away
Without so much as a groan
Struggling to find water
Never able to get food
With mud for bricks and mortar
Their buildings are rough and crude
These people die every day
Their lives in the hands of disease
How can we even think to say
That we're ill because of a sneeze
All of their life is a chore
Every day is a fight
And when they can't take anymore
There will be one tiny ray of light
Hope is what keeps them going
It helps them to be strong
They live their lives hoping
That a miracle will come along.

Rebecca Crowther (11)
Sale Grammar School, Sale

Great Minds

Van Nistelrooy scores a goal,
Into the net the ball then rolls,
Then he goes to celebrate,
Because his goals are always great,
His great mind can get the ball soaring
And the crowds will never stop roaring!

Robbie Mackay (12)
Sale Grammar School, Sale

The Haunted Mansion

Spooky and eerie,
The haunted mansion lies,
All dark and scary,
I hear its silent cries.

Deep in the valley,
Entwined with thorns,
This mansion stands,
Looking forlorn.

One hundred thousand years have passed,
Where spooks have lived with bats and rats,
I hear the screeches of the ghosts,
Whilst running away from the witches' croaks.

Troubled and tormented,
The dwellers abide,
By the curse of the haunted mansion,
I still hear its silent cries.

Charlotte Birkmire (13)
Sale Grammar School, Sale

Small

Away from the noise,
Up high in the sky,
The cars look like ants,
Scurrying by.

The tops of the buildings,
Look smaller down there
And as for the people,
Too small to compare.

It looks like a picture,
With lights flashing bright,
Like stars in the sky,
Standing out in the night.

Eleanor Titley (12)
Sale Grammar School, Sale

Hippos!

Hippos are smelly,
Hippos don't smile,
If I saw one, I'd run a mile!

Hippos are vicious,
Hippos are strong,
I'd be surprised to see a hippo sing a song!

Hippos are lazy,
Hippos will roar!
Hippos resemble a huge wild boar.

Hippos are clumsy,
Hippos are fat,
But hippos are cute and that's the end of that!

But if hippos are all of these things,
How come nobody likes them?

Helen Aylott (13)
Sale Grammar School, Sale

A World Of Care

What is this world so full of care?
We have no time to stand and stare,
Listening to the wind whistling through the trees,
The sound of people, the birds and the bees,
We all need to learn how to share,
In this world so full of care!

What do you want to achieve in life?
Whatever it is, it's up to you,
Great minds are best that's nothing new!

Are you ever all alone?
Standing there all on your own,
Your great mind will reassure,
Sweeping you up off the floor!

Matthew Volp (12)
Sale Grammar School, Sale

Autumn

Summer's going, winter's coming,
Autumn falls between,
The days are getting shorter
And the sun begins to fade.

The leaves start to change colours,
Green gives way to the reds, golds and browns,
The richness shines like fire in the sun,
Autumn has made its entrance.

Now the leaves begin to fall,
They crunch beneath your feet,
Children collecting conkers
And kicking all the leaves.

Everything looks different now,
All the trees are bare,
The weather has gone grey and wet
And the sun is becoming low.

Autumn's nearly over now,
Winter takes its place,
Time to say goodbye to conkers,
Snow will soon be falling.

Katy Figgess (11)
Sale Grammar School, Sale

The Motorbike

His wrist turned,
The power increased,
He gained speed, faster and faster,
He overtook us on the outside lane,
He revved up again and again,
The sun shone on that gleaming machine,
Oh so powerful clean and mean,
How I wish that it was mine,
As that motorbike drove by.

Tom Harrison (11)
Sale Grammar School, Sale

An Autumn Day

I wake up in the morning to find the lawn covered in leaves,
With all those bare looking trees,
All the school kids walking past,
With zipped up coats, scarves and woolly hats.

I walk outside to find I can see my breath,
With all the frost on the floor
And condensation on the door,
My fingers feeling like they are going to fall off.

Looking up at the sky,
I can see it's so white,
All clouds up there,
No star in sight.

I change my mind about going out,
I take off my gloves, scarf, hat and coat,
I go and make a fire and drink a cup of tea,
I prefer watching inside and keeping the house warm for me.

Amy Yates (13)
Sale Grammar School, Sale

Looking Around Space

Seen from space,
The Earth is like a multicoloured beach ball
Unmoving in the middle of nowhere

The clouds are like soft, gentle handfuls of cotton wool,
Swirling about in the breeze
And the stars are like shining pieces of glass a million miles away.

Seen from space,
The sun is like a gigantic ball of blazing fire,
That burns forever.

Alex Smallwood (11)
Sale Grammar School, Sale

My Little Sister

My little sister is like a summer's day,
Warm, bright and puts a smile on my face.

My little sister was born in the month of May,
When she walks with me she finds it hard to keep up with my pace.

My little sister has locks of curly black hair,
She has no homework, she only knows how to play.

When we go out, other people think she's so cute, so they
like to stare,
When she goes to playgroup she plays with modelling clay.

She thinks she's a boy because she plays on my Xbox,
She has teddy bear picnics with my little brother's Action Man.

She's so funny, she even sneaks on my little brother's socks,
She's so cute, I'm her number one fan.

Naim Rahman (11)
Sale Grammar School, Sale

Great Minds

Great minds think alike, that's what they always say,
But how can you really tell the difference at the end of the day?

They said Einstein was great, Shakespeare too,
But they can't be as good as me or you!

I'm good at maths, English, PE,
But what about science and history?

We're supposed to be equal, but can we really?
Who's as good as Shakespeare, not Rosie, not me!

I suppose, that's what it means, is that we're good at different things,
Whether it's science, law or even making gold rings!

Great minds think alike, I know what that means!
We *all* have great minds, no matter what it seems!

Rebecca Bennett (13)
Sale Grammar School, Sale

Love

Love is no ordinary thing
It affects everyone
And it is not just as in love
It can be friendship

But love in a couple
Is different it means more
There is hidden depth
One loves the other
They both love each other

Friendship is a bond
It is the way people can share problems
Can talk without being worried
Building a friendship is hard
Slowly it builds
And becomes strong.

Robert Poole (14)
Sale Grammar School, Sale

On A Crescent Bay

On a cliff I stood
And down I looked,
On a crescent bay.
The sun like a ball of fire,
Shone on the golden beach,
On a crescent bay.
People like ants fast and small,
The sea like a worm slowly moving,
On a crescent bay.
Looking down from a cliff,
Like a painting of a beach,
On a crescent bay.

Faye Griffin (11)
Sale Grammar School, Sale

Invisible Home

I wonder . . .
How can things so delicate and fine be so strong?
Almost invisible and fine when wet,
Capturing prey into its very own net,
Glistening with the raindrops,
Swaying with the breeze,
An invisible home that nobody sees.

An engineering masterpiece,
Created from within,
Beautiful but deadly,
To those who dare to venture in.

Spun with wondrous beauty,
Who knows how long it takes,
Wiped away in a second,
The web the spider makes.

Rachel Colwell (12)
Sale Grammar School, Sale

My Friends

My friends are so special to me,
I know they'll always be by my side.
They cheer me up when I feel sad,
We always find something to laugh about
And they never make me mad.

My friends are like my family,
I know them all so well.
I've only known them for over a year,
But it seems like I've known them all my life,
When they're around there's nothing to fear.

My best friends,
I don't know what I'd do without them.

Nicola Dragun (12)
Sale Grammar School, Sale

A Great Mind

I have picked a man who changed the world,
In a scribble of a pen,
One man who wrote and wrote,
Until it was his end.

Some stories turned to plays
And some are now still tales,
Others remade to films today,
In the honour of himself.

We think back to this man,
As famous as before,
The most popular of all good writers,
Since the day that he was born.

A good son to mother Mary
And so loyal to father John,
With seven brothers and sisters,
Who knew that he would be the one . . .

Known as Shakespeare.

Sarah Hoye (11)
Sale Grammar School, Sale

Great Minds

People with great minds,
Never find the time
To show them off,
Or use them in a special way,
They are too busy working them.

Everyone has a great mind,
Those that work hard, those that are kind,
Talent with animals, talent with maths,
Everyone has some special grasp,
Politicians, cleaners, bin men, judges.

Great minds don't always think alike.

Carys Templer (12)
Sale Grammar School, Sale

The Great Mind We Own

Historians speak of inventors,
Historians speak of mathematicians,
Historians speak of explorers,
But does anyone realise?

Scientists speak of other scientists,
Teachers teach about the great rulers of the world,
Doctors speak of great survivors, who bring to us lifesavers,
But does anyone realise?

We do a million things per second,
We all argue over who can multi-task,
None of us realise that every breath,
Every step, movement we make
Is created by one thing, *our great mind!*

William Goodman (11)
Sale Grammar School, Sale

The Shadow

Every movement,
Every step
Is followed in perfect synchrony,
All it takes is a little light,
For an identical form to follow you,
What could it be?

A demon chasing you everywhere,
Seeing all you do,
Wherever you go,
You cannot hide,
You are followed by this formidable shape,
What could it be?
The shadow.

Matthew Heeks (11)
Sale Grammar School, Sale

The Wanderer

No one knows his name,
He sneaks around at night, this king of the alleys,
He watches in the dark, his eyes flash in the headlights
of a passing car,
His wild black coat as dark as coal, soft to the touch,
But no one has had that honour,
For if you dared, his claws sharp as a knife,
Would slice your hand, no hesitation.
People who've seen him call him the wanderer,
By chance I saw him prowling around, doing his usual thing.
Suddenly a bat flew over his head,
Like a lightning flash, a swipe of a paw,
He caught it in mid-air.
The stealth hunter, proudly weaved his way
Dodging the shadows, disappeared into the inky darkness.
A majestic and mysterious moggy,
This feral feline, the wanderer nevertheless.

Charlie Gibson (11)
Sale Grammar School, Sale

What Makes A Great Mind?

G reat minds change the world,
R escuing us from questions and queries,
E xcelling in science, maths, art and English,
A great mind will change our lives,
T o something more brilliant and fun.

M aking something completely new for me and you,
I nteresting gizmos and gadgets for us,
N asty problems turned into a goldmine of ideas,
D aring to be different to change our planet,
S trength in the mind, not in the muscles!

Sean Barron (12)
Sale Grammar School, Sale

Ice Rink

So many different people from so many different places,
Skating here and there in so many different directions.
So many people joined up together,
Faster and faster, round and round the rink.
Laughing together, falling down together, having fun.
Smiling, shouting, enjoying themselves, skating in any and
every way, messing around.
People practising their moves, training, perfecting their skill.
Cold and icy, freezing fingers, bumps and bruises.
Exciting, joyous, noisy, fun,
Like everyone's Christmas wish.

Now it's empty,
All and any vibrance gone,
Walls collapsing, bricks falling down together, clouds of dust.
So many similar bricks like so many similar new places.
Just plain houses; just empty pavements, just lonely roads.
There's none left.
Nothing!

Rosie Peters (12)
Sale Grammar School, Sale

The Witch's Lair

Deep, deep down in the middle of the wood,
Lives a wicked, wicked witch,
Her hair is green with fury
And her eyes, you don't want to know!
Her house, if you dare enter, is filled with magic potions,
Cauldrons, spells all round, will surely freak you out
And if not, I'll tell you something that will really make you shout!
If you get too close, she'll eat you,
If you're too far away, she'll scream,
So let me tell you something, stay away from
The wicked witch!

Amy Vincent (11)
Sale Grammar School, Sale

Why War?

Why is this world full of fright, fear and worry?
Surely this is not meant to be.
God wanted it to be cheerful and friendly,
Not ruled by war.

In many countries violence dominates the streets.
People are scared even in their own homes.
Gunshots, blood, death all around them.

No longer can disputes be settled . . . without violence,
No longer can we watch the news . . . without war,
No longer can we live our lives without unnecessary death.
We seem to be living in a never-ending nightmare,
We will be living in fear up until we die.

But why?
What has happened to a normal compromise?
Why can't we live peacefully alongside each other?
Settle it with a great mind, not a violent mind.

Sam Wormald (13)
Sale Grammar School, Sale

More Time

What is this world if without care,
We need more time to stand and stare,
To glare and sit and watch whatever,
To lay and drink and worship trees,
Great minds will never think alike,
Otherwise they would have all invented the bike,
Great minds are not those with a high IQ,
They're people with a certain skill,
You could be starting right from nil,
Or you could be so smart you need a pill,
But do not sweat because whatever,
You have a great mind,
So don't let anyone tell you anything different,
Ever, ever.

James McParland (12)
Sale Grammar School, Sale

Two Worlds

What have you got on your Christmas list this year?
Writing to Santa, children make it quite clear!

A bike with suspension and a shiny new frame,
A PlayStation 2 with a brand new game.
Lipsticks and eyeshadows, blushers and gloss,
Sweet smelling perfumes, Lynx and Hugo Boss.
This year's latest fashion, faded jeans and mini skirts,
Calvin Klein and Miss Sixty, my God, how the prices hurt.

Rain to shower down on our thirsty fields of fields,
Rice and healthy vegetables, just a little more to eat.
A safe place to sleep without soldiers at the door,
With innocent people being killed no more.
An old pair of sandals to guard my burning feet,
A little shelter to shield us form the midday heat.

Don't these two worlds seem so far apart?
Aren't we all born with the same loving heart?
How could the world turn out so bad?
Death and destruction, has everyone gone mad?

Alex Turner (12)
Sale Grammar School, Sale

Winged Terror

It flew down from the mountain, all fury and power,
With its wings stretched outward on this dark and dismal hour.

You could see the strength of its scales and the temper in its skin,
As it opened its jaw, seeing the reddish flames within.

It burst its flames right out, onto my men,
Causing death, destruction and mayhem.

As we regrouped the last of our troops, loading our bows,
It swept down on us, like a flock of crows.

As we raised our crossbows up, ready to fire,
Killing the dragon was our only desire.

Ty Buckingham (11)
Sale Grammar School, Sale

What Makes A Great Mind?

What makes a great mind?
I don't really know.
A great mum? Who knows how to look after her young?
A great scientist? Who finds new solutions for things?
A great teacher? Who teaches their pupils everything they know?
A great doctor? Who treats people's illnesses?
What is a great mind?
I don't really know.
A great doctor, scientist, teacher, mum,
Are all people who have great minds.
Nevertheless everybody,
Each one of you
Has a mind - a great one too!

Emma Bagshaw (12)
Sale Grammar School, Sale

Stop And Stare

If you stop for a moment
And stand quite still,
You might see a deer
Lurking on a near hill.

If you turn over the soil
And stand quite still,
You might see a robin
With a soil-brown bill.

If you crawl on the ground
And lie quite still,
You might see a seal
The colour of snow.

So if you take a minute
Just to look,
You might see something
You never would've thought.

Victoria Horrocks (12)
Sale Grammar School, Sale

The Flying Queen

Diving
Swooping
Free as the majestical wind
Riding the air current
Surveying its mighty kingdom
From high above
What more could it ask for?

Then like a bolt of lighting
Out of its burrow comes a timid rabbit
Like a rock the bird plummets towards the earth
The rabbit looks up and takes its final breath
Then . . .
Death

Ripping and tearing at the carcass
The silent hunter casts a hooded glare at the scavengers
Hoping to get a scrap of flesh
Then as soon as she'd landed, she was off again
Diving . . .
Swooping . . .
Soaring . . .

Ben Daniels (11)
Sale Grammar School, Sale

My Lonely Thoughts

She chose to speak her mind though others could not tell
If she was feeling lonely or if she was feeling well
But somewhere deep inside her in a corner of a room
There was an answer deep inside her, an answer to her gloom
Her heart let out a cry of sorrow and regret
Her eyes burst with tears which made her jumper wet
Her lungs swept in a gust of air and a weak and weary smile
She sat there all alone, alone for a while.

Alis Thomas-Mellor (11)
The Belvedere School, Liverpool

Chocolate Temptations

The school bell is about to ring, I'll soon be going home.
I'll see the scrumptious chocolates, my mind forms a mind of its own!

The shining of the wrapper, it just catches my eye.
They all look delicious, which one shall I try?

Which one shall I choose? Which one has the nicest taste?
I like them all equally, I hate chocolate waste!

I finally make my decision, I go for the caramel,
I bite into the centre, the snapping sound of the shell!

My hand reaches out another time, it comes back with a diplomat,
Sugar-coated almonds and sauce that makes you fat!

Now I've had a dozen, only another dozen to go,
My mind wants the coconut bubbly, my stomach is saying *no!*

Oh go on, just one more, I've only got stomach ache,
Besides, one or two more chocolates, what problems can they make?

I think I'll have a Walnut Whip, it's left there all alone,
But what about the cherry cup? It will have to have a home!

Oh stomach, please be quiet, you're getting fed up, aren't you?
I've only got the coffee left, oh, and the strawberry chew!

Beside the creaminess of the strawberry, the sweet sensation
that you get!
The bitterness of the coffee, there's nothing like it yet!

It seems a shame to leave them there, the hazel and the
Turkish delight,
The great taste that reaches your taste buds, come on,
you know I'm right.

Oh please be quiet stomach, only two more for me to eat,
Besides the raspberry ripple is very hard to beat!

The sauce inside the chocolate, very thin and creamy,
Melting in my mouth, it tastes as sweet as honey!

Getting to the last one, can't eat this one fast!
Chocolate fudge, my favourite, got to make it last!

No more chocolates in the tray, I couldn't possibly eat anymore!
Now I am in chocolate pain, I was in chocolate galore!

Natalie Chaffe (13)
The Belvedere School, Liverpool

A Child's Wish List

(For her community)

Parks with green grass, flowers and no rubbish
Not empty sweet wrappers and dog mess, I wish
Supervised play areas with ice cream vans
Not having to play with runaway cans

Table tennis, rounders, football, the lot
The chance should be available from when we're tots
Walls should be left plain
As graffiti is not a game

More opportunities for young mums and dads
They may not have succeeded before, but still deserve a chance
If *they* don't know any better
How will they teach us children to be clever?

The capital of culture should do a lot of good
To people who will benefit, it really, really should
Different people, races, united as one
Seeing each other as equals with a strong bond

There were millions of pounds awarded to Liverpool
It should also benefit my community as
It's the heart of the jewel.

Saadiqa Salisu (13)
The Belvedere School, Liverpool

Fear Of The Angels

We've opened up careful
Not very realistic holes in the
Fabric of the universe (time, space, the lot)
And the careful, humdrum existence of me and all my
Plans and ambitions have been thrown to infinity like
Glossy magazines in recycle bins, we were not born to be *told* what
To be by the people who turn us inside on ourselves
This is not the world I was made to believe in
Time dances its dance and I can count those who are with me
On one hand

You always added up your sums with your hair all full of
Pink-purple sadness, caught the sunshine down into those
Little cotton handbags, you, so out of character, dragged
                                    around with you
You've gone from one game to another and left the rest to us
Spinning in the middle you moved so fast, and no one can run
                                    like you can run
And no one can curl those little confusions to whips and chains
Like you always could

Did you find your pretty silence through worrying us all?
Or was it always just about you and the way your mind made you die
This was never our world, but I think I have found it now
Belonging to someone that you can become if I
Jump from the roofs and miss the ground

Minute changes, minute footsteps, nobody saw us
Fall from Heaven because we never flew that high for fear
Of the angels.

Ruth Davies (14)
The Belvedere School, Liverpool

Where Is It?

Rainbow, rainbow,
Where could it be?
Where is it?
I cannot see.

Over the hills?
Beside the church?
Where is it?
I'll need to search.

I looked around,
But still no luck,
Where is it?
Behind that duck?

It's taking so long,
It begins to rain,
Where is it?
Oh, what a shame.

The rain continues
And the sun has come out,
'Where is it?'
I began to shout.

The clouds disappear,
The rain begins to stop,
Where is it?
It comes out with a . . . *pop!*

Margaret Huang (11)
The Belvedere School, Liverpool

The Wolf's Cry

The wolf scampered through the thick black wood,
Howling and yelping as loud as she could,
The jet-black demon was catching up on her,
The demon set fire to all the trees there.

The wolf was terrified, distraught and lonely,
If she hadn't stole his precious jewel if only, if only,
The demon was going to kill her and all of her kind,
No mercy would be given, their paws would be tied.

Suddenly, she thought of a plan,
A sharp left she turned and ran, and ran,
She jumped down a quarry to the demon's surprise
And landed on a ledge invisible to the eye.

The demon scoured the top of the quarry,
He walked off, if he had feelings, he would have felt sorry,
She ran up the steep hill,
Now she had the jewel she had freed her people.

Georgie Clark (11)
The Belvedere School, Liverpool

Silence In The Dark

You can hear, the silence in the dark
Breaking through the darkness like the singing of a lark
Cutting through the air like a swift slicing knife
Like the never-ending struggle in this game we call life

Listen in the silence and you will hear
As everything in life becomes crystal clear
Is there ever truly silence, in a world so full of sound?
From all the people chatting, to them wandering all around

You can almost feel the silence in the darkness now
Swallowing the sound if we will allow
Stop, as you are walking through the park
And you might hear, the silence, in the dark.

Kristina Mills (11)
The Belvedere School, Liverpool

The Seasons

Flowers skip hand in hand
Trees sway as they stand
Sun smiles on the Earth
Plants are waiting for birth
Spring's here

Sun breathes warm here
Leaves singing softly near
The world buzzing loud
Nature watches proud
Summer's here

The rain runs along the floor
It eats the dry ground on the moor
Rain jumps, it bounces high
Clouds shuffle in the sky
Autumn's here

The snow begins life with frost
Grass drowns, the green is lost
Trees shiver, branches bare
The coldness dances in the air
Winter's here.

Nneka Cummins (11)
The Belvedere School, Liverpool

Culture City

L iving in Liverpool
I s really great,
V ery lucky to have won
E uropean Capital of Culture 2008.
R aces of every kind live here,
P oets, singers, people who are smart.
O ptimistic, happy people,
O h and people who do art.
L ive in Liverpool and play your part!

Amy Giblin (12)
The Belvedere School, Liverpool

Locked Up

I'm locked up in a box,
There's no light I can see.
I'm locked up in a box,
In the strangest place as can be.

I'm locked up in a box,
With feelings so blue.
I'm locked up in a box,
There's nothing I can do.

I'm locked up in a box,
There isn't a sound, not a peep.
I'm locked up in a box,
I can't even sleep.

I'm locked up in a box,
With nothing to eat.
I'm locked up in a box,
I could die for some meat.

I'm locked up in a box,
I think I am dying.
I'm locked up in a box,
I just can't help crying.

I'm locked up in a box,
I shall pass away.
I'm locked up in a box
And here is where I stay.

Melissa Huang (12)
The Belvedere School, Liverpool

The Lane

I'd like to tell you about Lark Lane
Sometimes it can be a bit of a pain
The noise some nights is absolutely mad
And we can blame it on some of the lads

You've got Thorough Goods and a shop that sells pine
And if you're looking for somewhere to wine and dine,
There's Greek, Italian, Chinese too,
Hamburgers, hot dogs, try them, please do!

So, take your girl or your boy,
Go to the lane and enjoy,
Needless to say,
You'll have a great day,
Or a really good night,
When you're out on
Lark Lane!

Frances Murphy (11)
The Belvedere School, Liverpool

The Monster's Lair

On the top of a hill
A monster lies and gives everyone a thrill

With a snarl on his face
In a desolate place

He lurks around
Making a dreary sound

In his sunless, sulphurous lair
He stomps around without a care

He lives in a dank lair
And no one dare go there!

Demi McIntosh (11)
The Belvedere School, Liverpool

A Flower

A flower is as bright and
As beautiful as the sun
Reflecting off a stained glass
Window in a church

It has an individual scent
Like the aroma surrounding
A perfume shop in the middle
Of a high street

Each and every flower is
Unique with distinguishing
Features to separate it from
Other species of flower

There are all sorts of
Flowers around the world
I am a flower
So are you.

Michelle Young (12)
The Belvedere School, Liverpool

Nature In Spring

Caterpillars munch on tangy leaves,
Whereas the slug on the grass leaves slimy grease.
The trees sway from side to side,
While the wind sweeps down the slide.

It's the time when the chick opens its wings,
Open its orange beak, then sings.
It's the time when the waters become smooth and light,
Getting the glow of the pure moonlight.

Everything is silent and dark,
But then the seagulls gives a big *squawk!*
The dormouse tucked back in
And the eagle swooped over the bin.

The flowers shine in the dark,
Where honeybees love to park.
Nature goes perfect in spring,
It makes you feel agile and your body goes *ting!*

Trina Banerjee (11)
The Blue Coat School, Liverpool

Paradise: Only In My Dreams

There's a place called Paradise,
But it's only in my dreams.
The world is changing,
Ripped and torn at the seams;
There's a place called Paradise,
But it's only in my dreams
And now, destroyed towers
Are replaced by laser beams;
There's a place called Paradise,
But it's only in my dreams.
The world and what it's like
Is different from what it seems;
There's a place called Paradise,
But it's only in my dreams.
Innocent men and women are sent to war,
To live in extremes;
There's a place called Paradise,
But it's only in my dreams
And beautiful rainforests, ruined
For a few stupid reams;
There's a place called Paradise,
But it's only in my dreams.
To search for paradise,
Is all very well,
But to live here in Heaven,
Is to realise what is Hell.

Jack Kenny (12)
The Blue Coat School, Liverpool

The Beggar Man

What do I say to the beggar man
Holding out his scrawny hat?
Do I say, 'Be gone you pest,'
And spit where all the rich have spat?

I could just give a coin or two,
To turn away that staring face,
That thinks I must be filthy rich
Because I hold a black briefcase.

I could well give a little more,
Enough to buy a little food
And, perhaps a brisk hello,
Just to show that I'm not rude.

But what's the point of being 'nice',
It wastes my time and helps him not,
All are civil and he is sad
And so his heart begins to rot.

I should give more than just loose cash
And should not act so rudely coy,
It's not just change that I can give,
I can give him a little joy.

After all he's still a man
And worthy of a man's respect,
I'll speak to him as if a friend
And won't his empty hat neglect.

Peter Davey (16)
The Blue Coat School, Liverpool

The Traveller

I am the traveller,
Merry as can be,
Just wind me up upon a path
And then just set me free.

I am the traveller,
I ramble, amble, roam,
I never think of stopping,
On my back I carry my home.

I am the traveller,
Never weary, tired or sad,
You may just be able to call me,
A bit of a wandering lad.

I am the traveller,
Nature is my mate,
My favourite gift of all would be,
The whole world on a plate.

I am the traveller,
Inspired by life to live,
If I was to give a gift to you,
The world would be what I would give.

I am the traveller,
I gaze in awe at the world,
I especially love just watching,
All natural wonders unfurled.

I am the traveller,
When I left years and years ago,
The hustle and bustle of city life,
Like a river I did flow.

Helena Sweeney (11)
The Blue Coat School, Liverpool

This Perfect State

Oh to be asleep! Those precious little hours,
'Tween moon bidding the stars goodnight
And th'uplifting chirps of nature's morn,
Escaping reality, subconscious powers,
Wander far, far away from sight,
To the place where all my dreams are born.

Dare I drift into deep delusions by night,
Or gaze into sunlit reveries?
I float and fall into oceans vast of dreams,
When my mind empowered cannot but excite,
These surreal moments are nothing but lies,
A simple illusion of sleep, it seems.

But still, I dream of sensual sunsets, while
Deep seas kiss the heavenly artist's sky,
Sensual sunsets soon become a senseless sunrise,
The marathon of dreams enters its final mile.
As distant sounds draw near, still I lie,
Harsh realities of life run from my open eyes.

Amidst awakening, I wonder why,
These dreams of utopia and perfect bliss,
Seem so far from my imminent fate.
I close my eyes and look to the sky,
As life's long lane turns and twists,
Still, I lie in this perfect state.

Kieran O'Sullivan (17)
The Blue Coat School, Liverpool